Journeys

Direct Instruction Reading

Level 2
Textbook 3

Siegfried Engelmann
Owen Engelmann
Karen Lou Seitz Davis
Ann Arbogast

A Division of The McGraw-Hill Companies

Columbus, Ohio

Illustration Credits

Dan Clifford, Olivia Cole, Mark Corcoran, Kersti Frigell, John Edwards and Associates, Meryl Henderson, Benrei Huang, Susan Jerde, Jan Pyk, Pat Schories, Lauren Simeone, Jim Shough, Joel Snyder, and Gary Undercuffler.

SRA/McGraw-Hill
A Division of The **McGraw·Hill** *Companies*

Copyright © 2000 by SRA/McGraw-Hill. All rights reserved. Except as permitted under the United States Copyright Act, no part of this publication may be reproduced or distributed in any form or by any means, or stored in a database or retrieval system, without prior written permission from the publisher.

Printed in the United States of America.

Send all inquiries to:
SRA/McGraw-Hill
787 Orion Place
Columbus, OH 43240-4027

0-02-683536-3

5 6 7 8 9 VHJ 03 02 01 00

101

1. hadn't
2. where's
3. who's
4. there's

1. storm
2. hurt
3. know
4. knew
5. curled
6. waited

1. station
2. bother
3. brother
4. kitchen
5. warm

1. early
2. noti<u>ce</u>
3. pupp<u>ies</u>
4. dreaming
5. remembered
6. sno<u>wy</u>

Dot and Dud
Part Three

Dud was trying to go north, but he went south. He went very close to the ranger station. But he didn't see it and went right on past it. The snow was coming down so hard that he couldn't see the station, and he was so lazy that he didn't bother sniffing with his nose. So Dud passed up that station and went up a mountain to the south of the station. At last he came to a large ski lodge where there were many people.

Dud did not know where he was, but he said to himself, "There are people here, so there must be a kitchen around here." Dud found the kitchen very quickly by sniffing for the smells of ham and eggs.

Then Dud put on a little act. He sat outside the kitchen and made little barks. "Ruff, ruff." When a woman opened the door, he wagged his tail and tried to look very friendly, but also very cold.

"What are you doing out here?" the woman said. "You poor dog. You must be very hungry and tired. Come in here."

She led Dud inside and gave him a lot of soup and a big pile of meat scraps. This was like a dream for Dud. He ate everything and then took a wonderful nap right next to the big, warm stove. He was one happy dog.

But while he was snoozing, things were not going well for the other dogs. Dot had found the trail of the lost mountain climber, but in the snow storm, the other dogs could not keep up with her. She followed the trail up slopes that were so steep that she kept slipping. Once she slipped and slid down a long way. Dot got up and kept trying until she reached a rocky place where the mountain climber was sitting. He was hurt and couldn't walk. He just sat there with his eyes closed. Dot knew that he was in bad shape.

She barked and howled as loud as she could, but the sound of her barks did not go far in the thick falling snow. The other dogs were over a mile away, and they did not hear anything. Dot didn't know what to do, so she curled up next to the mountain climber to keep him warm. Then she waited, and waited, and waited. It was getting close to night time.

More to come.

Not all fish in the sea look the same. You can tell where a fish lives by the shape of the fish. Fish that live near the shore are shaped like this. The shape of these fish lets them turn quickly.

Fish that live in the open water look like this. The shape of these fish lets them go very fast.

Some fish that live in the open water hunt other fish. They have to be fast. Sometimes they come near the shore and hunt fish shaped like this. The fish near the shore are good at getting away from the hunting fish.

1. Do all fish that live in the sea have the same shape?

2. Where do fish with this shape live?

3. Where do fish with this shape live?

4. Which fish can turn quickly, fish that live near the shore or fish that live in the open water?

5. Which fish can swim very fast?

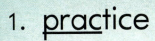

1. <u>pr</u>actice
2. <u>fi</u>nish
3. <u>to</u>morrow
4. <u>some</u>where

1. sta<u>tion</u>
2. na<u>tion</u>
3. ques<u>tion</u>
4. ac<u>tion</u>
5. mo<u>tion</u>

1. right
2. slight
3. quietly
4. quickly

1. earl<u>y</u>
2. know<u>ing</u>
3. <u>n</u>o<u>ti</u>c<u>e</u>d
4. <u>pupp</u>ies
5. snow<u>y</u>
6. <u>p</u>low<u>ing</u>

Dot and Dud
Part Four

That evening, while Dud was sleeping in the kitchen and dreaming of summer time, a truck pulled up to the ski lodge. The head ranger came inside to pick up Dud. The cook had called the ranger station and told them that one of their dogs was at the lodge.

The ranger was not happy. He led Dud to the truck and put him in the back with the other work dogs. They were coming back from the north mountains. They had not found the mountain climber, and they hadn't found Dot. The ranger wanted to come home before it got too dark. He planned to go out again early in the morning.

When Dud got in the truck, he didn't know that Dot was somewhere on the mountain. But right away, he knew that something was wrong. The other dogs didn't start complaining about Dud getting lost. Those dogs didn't even look at him. They just looked down at the floor.

Dud tried to talk to the other dogs. "Did you find the mountain climber?" he asked. The other dogs didn't say a thing. They just looked down.

Dud said, "You know, I had some wonderful soup at the ski lodge, and I . . ."

"Be quiet," the oldest dog said.

Dud was quiet for a while. Then he noti<u>ce</u>d that Dot was not in the truck. "Where's Dot?" he asked.

"Lost," one of the work dogs said.

"What do you mean?" Dud asked. "Where is she?"

"Somewhere on the mountain," the oldest dog said.

"Do you mean she's out there alone?"

Some of the dogs said, "Yes," very quietly.

Dud loved Dot. He didn't always show it, but he loved her. As he sat in the back of that truck, he remembered her from way back, when Dot and Dud were little puppies. When any other puppy would pick on Dud, Dot always stuck up for him. Dud remembered a lot of other things as the truck went down that snowy road. He remembered how sad he had been when he and Dot had to leave their mother. The only good thing about going to the ranger station was that Dot was with him.

More to come.

Once there was a rabbit who always bragged about how fast she was. One day, when the rabbit was bragging, a little mole said, "I will race you."

The rabbit laughed and laughed. "I will race you anytime," the rabbit said.

"Fine," the mole said. "Be here at one o'clock at night. And if you do not win the race, you will stop bragging."

The rabbit agreed.

That night, the rabbit and the mole were ready to start the race. Many other animals were there to watch the race, too, but it was so dark that most of the animals couldn't see. The mole said, "Ready, set, go," and both animals started to run.

Did the rabbit win the race? No. She didn't even finish the race, because she couldn't see. She ran into a rock. She heard bells and saw stars. Now she doesn't brag. She thinks she's a mole named Bill.

1. What kind of animal bragged?

2. Who said he would race the rabbit?

3. When did the race start?

4. Why didn't the rabbit win?

5. Now the rabbit thinks she is a ▆▆▆▆▆.

1. vacation
2. mention
3. fraction
4. action
5. nation

1. lowered
2. licked
3. lowering
4. darkness
5. plowing

1. clinic
2. question
3. practice
4. finish

1. trouble
2. slight
3. doctor
4. tomorrow

Dot and Dud
Part Five

Dud was in the back of the ranger's truck, remembering how much he loved Dot. All at once, he said, "No, she can't be lost." Then he turned to the oldest dog and asked, "Why did you leave her out there?"

"She'll be all right, if we find her early in the morning."

Dud said, "But what about the mountain climber? Won't he freeze if he stays out there much longer?"

All the other dogs looked down.

Dud didn't say anything more to the other dogs. But he said something to himself. He said, "If they can't find her, I'll find her." Dud was not talking the way he sometimes did when he said, "I'll be better." This was not a game.

   The truck stopped in front of the ranger station. As soon as the ranger opened the back door, Dud jumped out and ran as fast as he could. The ranger shouted, "Dud, come back here. It's dark out there."

   The other dogs barked and yelled at him. Dud knew where he was going—north.

Pretty soon some of the other dogs started to follow Dud. Then all of them followed. Then the ranger followed. Away they went, plowing through the deep snow up the mountain. Dud said to himself, "I know Dot's smell better than anyone else's in the world. I will find that smell. I will. I will."

He put his nose in the snow and snorted and sniffed. He didn't even notice that the snow was cold. Again and again—snort, sniff, snort, sniff. Then he did it the fast way. He just put his nose in the snow and kept it there, like a snow plow, snorting and sniffing. And up the mountain he went, just as fast as he could run.

Suddenly, there was a very slight smell in the snow. It was Dot. Yes, yes, yes. It was Dot. "Come on," he barked to the other dogs. "Follow me."

And up the mountain he went once more, his head in the snow like a snow plow. When he came to steep parts and slid down, he just tried harder and did it again until he made it. Her smell was getting stronger and stronger.

More to come.

103

Jim was a snake that loved to eat bugs. He could eat and eat and eat. One year, there were lots of bugs, and Jim ate, and ate, and ate. But the more he ate, the fatter he got. Soon he was so fat that he could not sneak up on bugs. He wouldn't slide through the grass. He would plow through the grass. All the bugs would hear him coming. They would call to each other and say, "Here comes that fat snake again. Let's get out of here."

And they would.

Right now, Jim has not had a bug to eat in two weeks. He is not as fat as he was. He can slide through the grass better than he did before. But he is still too slow. He won't catch any bugs for another week. By then, he'll be a slim Jim.

1. What kind of animal is Jim?
2. What did he love to eat?
3. One year, there were a lot of ▬▬▬▬.
4. What happened to Jim after he ate and ate?
5. Could he sneak up on bugs any more?
6. How long will it be before he is a slim Jim?

ew oy tion aw   **104**

1. direct
2. direc<u>tion</u>
3. inform
4. informa<u>tion</u>
5. collect
6. collec<u>tion</u>

1. <u>b</u>oring
2. <u>sn</u>oring
3. <u>w</u>illing
4. <u>h</u>igher
5. <u>str</u>onger
6. <u>d</u>arkness

1. minutes
2. popular
3. either
4. except
5. wif*e*

1. through
2. thought
3. licked
4. curled
5. lowered
6. doctor

Dot and Dud
Part Six

Dud was leading the other dogs high into the mountains. He knew that he was getting very close to Dot because her smell was strong.

Suddenly Dud stopped and looked up. He had come to the rocky part where Dot was curled up next to the mountain climber. For a moment, Dud stood there and looked into the darkness. He could see Dot. He ran over, sat down next to her, and licked her nose. "Are you okay?" he asked.

"Yes," she said. "But I'm so glad you're here. I don't think the mountain climber can make it through the night."

Dot and Dud looked at each other and wagged their tails. Then Dud called to the other dogs, "Come up here. I found them."

In a little while, the ranger and the other dogs made it up the steep slope. The ranger had a little sled. He put the climber on the sled. He and the dogs lowered the sled down the steep slope. Then the dogs pulled the sled back to the ranger station.

After the ranger put the dogs in the kennel, he took the mountain climber to a doctor.

The dogs were very tired. They just ate a little bit and curled up in their beds. Dud was starting to fall asleep when the oldest dog said, "I want to thank Dud for doing what he did. He saved a mountain climber. And he did more than that."

All the other dogs looked up and waited for the oldest dog to say more. "He showed what he can do when he really puts his mind to it. He showed us that he's going to be pretty good at his job."

The other dogs said, "Yeah, pretty good."

Just then, the ranger came back and thanked the dogs. He left some meat scraps and a large ham bone. After the ranger left, the oldest dog picked up the ham bone and took it over to Dud. He said, "This is for you."

Dud started to say, "Well, I really don't think I should . . ." He was going to tell them that he shouldn't have the bone, but it smelled so good that he stopped talking and started to do something else. Yum, yum, yum.

The end.

Sharks are hunters of the sea. Sharks are fish, and they are very strong. But they are different from most fish. Most fish have teeth that are like your teeth and bones that are like your bones. Sharks do not have teeth like yours. The teeth of a shark are really just scales. The bones of sharks are not like your bones.

Real bone holds up the part of your nose near your face. Grab your nose near your face, just below your eyes. Move it from side to side. Does real bone bend?

The same stuff sharks' bones are made of holds up the tip of your nose. Grab the tip of your nose and move it from side to side. Do sharks' bones bend?

1. Are sharks fish?
2. The teeth of the shark are really ▬▬▬.
3. A shark's bones are made of the same stuff that holds up the tip of your ▬▬▬.
4. Does real bone bend?
5. Do sharks' bones bend?

1. <u>w</u>illing
2. <u>sn</u>oring
3. <u>b</u>oring
4. <u>ei</u>ther
5. <u>ex</u>cept
6. <u>p</u>olite

1. patient
2. certain
3. clinic
4. practi<u>ce</u>
5. trouble

1. Bill Wilson
2. Milly
3. minute
4. expert
5. asleep

1. popular
2. school
3. sure
4. wife
5. answer

Boring Bill
Part One

Bill Wilson was a nice man. He was kind to dogs, cats, and other animals. He took good care of his car, his house, and his lawn. He loved his wife, Milly, and he liked people. He was always willing to help people when they needed help, and he was very polite.

Bill Wilson did of all these nice things, but he still was not a very popular person. You see, Bill was boring. He was so boring that every time he started talking, he would put people to sleep. Within a few minutes, people would either be yawning or leaving the room. Within a few more minutes, anybody who stayed in the room would be snoring.

Bill once gave a talk to parents at a school. After only ten minutes, everybody except Bill was asleep. The room was very noisy because people were snoring so loudly. After the meeting, one woman said, "We were snoring because Bill is boring." From that day on, people called Bill Wilson "Boring Bill." They didn't say it to his face, but they said it. And Bill knew about it.

One evening, Bill said to his wife, "The more I speak, the more people sleep. There must be something I can do to be less boring, but I'm not sure what it is. Tell me, Milly, what should I do to be less boring?"

Milly didn't answer him, because she was sound asleep. Bill looked at her and said to himself, "I must do something to change the way I talk. I am tired of being so boring."

More to come.

105

Jen liked to make things, but the things she made didn't fit. Once she made a hat for her brother. That hat went over his ears, his eyes, his nose, his mouth, and his neck. He said, "This hat is so big, it could be a bag."

He cut three holes in it. One hole was on top. The other two holes were on the sides. He gave the hat to a little girl and said, "Here is a fine dress for you."

She loved that dress.

1. Who liked to make things?
2. Did the things she made fit well?
3. What did she make for her brother?
4. Was that hat too big or too small?
5. How many holes did he cut in the hat?
6. Now that hat is a ▇▇▇▇.

Boring Bill
Part Two

    Bill tried to say things that would interest other people. He asked questions and tried to get people to talk about themselves. He tried to say things that were funny. He tried to talk faster and louder. He tried to smile more when he talked. But all those changes made no difference. After Bill was through speaking, everybody else was sleeping.
    One day, Bill was at home. He was practicing in front of the mirror. He smiled, moved around a lot, and talked to the mirror.

Just then the door bell rang. Bill opened the door and saw a woman who said, "I am an expert at making people sleep. I work for the Sleep More Clinic. We help people who have trouble sleeping. I hear that you can make people sleep, too."

"Yes," Bill said. "If I speak for a while, people will sleep."

"That is interesting," the sleep expert said. "Can you explain how you make people sleep?"

"Yes, I can," Bill said. "It seems that I am boring." Bill went on to explain why he was boring and tell about some things that happened to him. When Bill finished explaining his problem, he noticed that the sleep expert was snoring.

Bill woke the expert up. The expert said, "Oh, dear. I don't know what came over me. I was listening to what you said, and then . . ."

Bill said, "Oh, I understand. That happens to me all the time."

The expert said, "Do you mind if I come back tomorrow with some other experts from the clinic?"

"No, I don't mind."

After the expert left, Bill made up his mind that he would be interesting when the others visited him. He said to himself, "They will not be able to fall asleep."

More to come.

I have four legs, two arms, and a back. I stand about four feet high, and I am made mostly of wood. My legs are stiff, and they hold me up.

I have a padded seat where people can sit. People rest their arms on my arms. I will stay where you put me, but I don't like to be left alone for a long time. Please sit on me.

1. What kind of thing is telling this story?
    • a car   • a chair   • a dog

2. Name the part that is padded.

3. What do people do with this thing?

4. What does this thing want you to do?

? ? ?

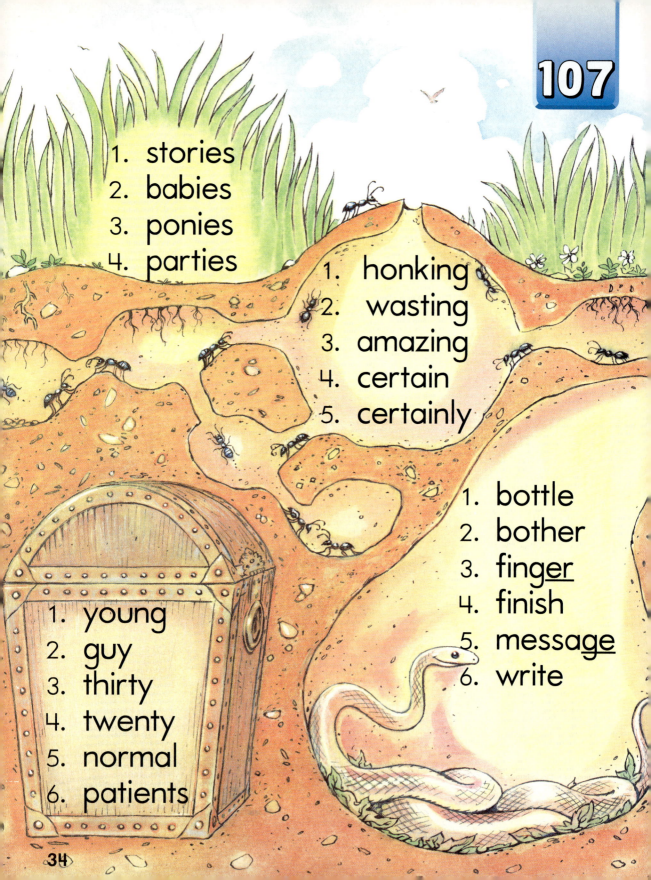

1. stories
2. babies
3. ponies
4. parties

1. honking
2. wasting
3. amazing
4. certain
5. certainly

1. young
2. guy
3. thirty
4. twenty
5. normal
6. patients

1. bottle
2. bother
3. fing<u>er</u>
4. finish
5. messa<u>ge</u>
6. write

Boring Bill
Part Three

Nine experts from the Sleep More Clinic were on their way to visit Bill. One of them kept arguing with the others. She said, "I don't believe those stories about how Bill is able to make people sleep. We know more about putting people to sleep than he knows. After all, we are experts. Bill is not an expert, so Bill can't know more about sleep than we know. I think we are wasting our time."

The woman who visited Bill the day before said, "We are not wasting our time."

The leader of the team said, "Now, now. Let's not argue. We'll listen to what Bill has to say. I want everybody to take notes and ask good questions."

When they got to Bill's place, they asked Bill to explain how he put people to sleep. He said, "When I talk in my normal voice, people just fall asleep. But today, I'm talking in a voice that will keep all of you wide awake. I have been working on this voice, and it is very interesting. It is not like my normal voice, which is soft and easy. This voice has a lot of bounce. I think you'll see that ..."

One of the experts said, "Zzzz."

Another expert said, "Snort, blub, zzzz."

The woman who believed that she knew more about putting people to sleep than Bill did said, "Gl gl honk zzzzzzzz."

Bill stopped talking and waited for the others to wake up. The first one to wake up was the leader. "Oh my," he said as he looked at the others. "That was amazing. You certainly do know how to put people to sleep."

After a while, all the experts except one were awake. The only one who kept on honking and snoring was the expert who thought she knew more about putting people to sleep than Bill did.

She woke up when the experts were getting ready to leave. She said, "Well, let's begin the meeting."

The leader said, "We're through meeting."

More next time.

There once was a big piece of ice that didn't like the cold. That ice was in an ice box. One day the ice said, "I'm tired of being cold. I will go where it is warm."

The other pieces of ice in the ice box said, "But if you go where it is warm, you will melt."

But the piece didn't listen to the others. That piece of ice left the ice box. Soon the piece noticed that it was getting smaller. The piece of ice said, "I must go back to the ice box."

And it did. Now the piece does not hate the cold. That piece says, "I am smaller but wiser."

1. What didn't the piece of ice like?

2. Where did the ice live?

3. Who tried to warn the piece of ice about leaving the ice box?

4. They told the big piece that it would ▇▇▇▇.

5. Did the piece of ice leave the ice box?

6. Did the piece of ice return to the ice box?

7. Is the piece of ice bigger or smaller?

Boring Bill
Part Four

When the nine experts from the Sleep More Clinic left Bill's place, he felt very sad. He had tried to be interesting, but his plan had not worked.

Later that day, Bill felt a lot better. He got a call from the leader of the team. The leader said, "Bill, could you come to the Sleep More Clinic tomorrow? You may be able to help us with some people who have not been able to sleep."

So the next morning at nine-thirty, Bill was at the clinic. The leader told Bill that the first patient he would see had not been able to sleep for three nights. When that patient came in, she said, "Nobody can help me sleep. What's the point of talking to another doctor? I know I won't sleep tonight either."

Bill said, "I'm not a doctor. I'm just a boring kind of guy."

The patient said, "So now I don't even get to talk to a doctor."

Bill said, "Well, you don't really have to talk. All you have to do is listen to what I say. I'll talk for a while, and before you know . . ."

"Snort. Zzzz."

The same thing happened with the next patient, a young woman who had not been able to sleep for nearly a week.

After Bill put the second patient to sleep, the leader said, "Why are we working with patients one at a time? Let's bring in all the other patients and see what happens."

So twenty patients came in. Bill talked to them for five minutes, and the room was filled with the sounds of people snorting, snoring, honking, and making lots of **Z**s. The sounds came from twenty patients with sleep problems and four doctors from the Sleep More Clinic who had been watching Bill work.

Before Bill left, the leader of the sleep team asked Bill, "Would you like to work at our clinic?"

We'll find out more next time.

108

   Steve wanted to climb a mountain. He didn't know which trail to take, but he was afraid to ask anyone. He didn't want people to think he wasn't smart. So he didn't ask any questions.

   Steve picked a trail and started up it. Soon the trail became steep and rocky. Before Steve knew it, he was standing on the edge of a cliff. Steve was stuck. So a ranger had to come with ropes to pull Steve off the cliff. The ranger said, "Why did you take that trail?" Steve didn't know what to say.

   Later Steve told himself, "Next time, I'll ask questions."

1. What did Steve want to climb?

2. Did Steve know which trail to take?

3. Did he ask anybody which trail to take?

4. Steve got stuck on a ▬▬▬▬.

5. Will Steve ask questions next time?

109

tion　aw　ou　sion　shion　ew

1. men<u>tion</u>
2. ac<u>tion</u>
3. vi<u>sion</u>
4. <u>nation</u>

1. island
2. added
3. size
4. inch
5. grown
6. maker

1. strange
2. regular
3. swerve
4. elevator

1. bear
2. giant
3. ago
4. using
5. father
6. full

45

Boring Bill
Part Five

Bill had a new job at the Sleep More Clinic, and Bill was the star sleep maker. He would work with people who couldn't sleep. After he talked to them for a few minutes, they were making Zs with big smiles on their faces.

Bill was the star, but he still had problems. One day, he started talking to people in the elevator. When he got off the elevator, everybody else was asleep. One time after work, he started talking to the bus driver as the bus moved along the street. Soon the bus started to swerve. The driver was asleep. Bill woke the driver up just in time.

Bill kept reading books about how to be interesting, and Bill kept trying different things. At last, he found something that worked. He talked in a high voice and talked faster. Nobody fell asleep. He could talk to the people in the elevator, and they wouldn't fall asleep. He could talk to bus drivers without putting them to sleep.

But Bill's high voice did not work with his patients. When he talked to them in his high voice, they just looked at him and said, "This is not working. I am still awake."

So now Bill has two voices. He talks in his regular voice when he is working with patients. But when he is not at work, he speaks in a high voice. That voice sounds a little strange, but it doesn't put his wife or his friends to sleep. In fact, Bill is pretty popular, and people no longer call him Boring Bill. They call him the Sleep Master.

The end.

109

Before the moose and the goose met, the moose was bothered because he had a bug on his back. That bug kept biting him. He tried many ways to get rid of the bug. He rolled in the dirt. He rubbed his back against trees. He dove under water. But none of the things the moose did stopped that bug from biting him.

At last the moose yelled, "I hate bugs."

The goose was walking by and heard the moose. The goose said, "I don't hate bugs. I love them."

That goose hopped up on the moose's back and ate the bug. That made the moose happy, and that made the goose happy. After that, the moose and the goose became good friends.

1. What kept biting the moose?
2. Who hated bugs?
3. Who loved bugs?
4. What did the goose do with the bug?
5. How did that make the moose feel?

A

1. Owen
2. using
3. island
4. ago
5. apart

B

1. pap<u>er</u>
2. t<u>o</u>re
3. grain
4. drift
5. size
6. inch

C

1. father
2. full
3. through
4. giant
5. bear

D

1. <u>bobb</u>ing
2. <u>pea</u>nut
3. <u>door</u>way
4. <u>class</u>room
5. <u>mess</u>ages

Owen, Fizz, and Liz
Part One

A long time ago, there were two islands that were almost the same in every way. They were the same size and the same shape. Both islands had a large beach on the north end. Both had a large mountain in the middle. Both had the same hills and the same valleys. But these islands were not in the same place. They were many, many miles apart.

Another thing that was not the same about these islands was the people who lived on them. On one island, there were ten little tiny people. These people were only about one inch tall. Some of the spiders on their island were bigger than they were. On the other island, there were three giants. They were almost twenty feet tall. They were so big that they could not walk through the doorway of your classroom. They would have to crawl in. And they would not be able to stand up after they got inside. These giants were so big and strong that they could pick up a bear and hold it like a puppy.

One day, one of the giants found a green bottle. To him, this bottle was very small. In fact, it was not as long as his finger. The giant who found the bottle had never seen a bottle before.

The giant's name was Owen, and the only people he had ever seen were the other two giants on the island. They were his father and mother. Owen was almost full grown. He was about as tall as his mother, but not as tall as his father.

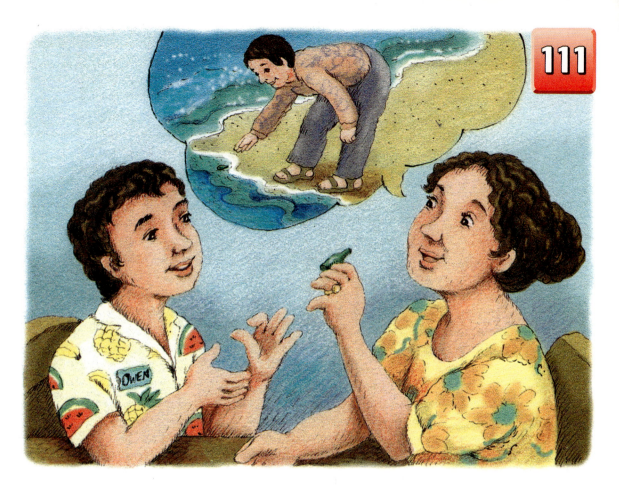

Owen picked up the bottle and looked at it for a long time. Then he took it home and showed it to his mother. "What is this thing?" he asked.

"That thing is a bottle," she said. Then she added, "I once heard that people can send messages to other people by using a bottle. They just write a note, put it in the bottle, and put the bottle in the water. The wind and the waves will take that bottle to another place that is far away. Somebody will find it washed up on the beach."

More to come.

Bottles are made from glass. Glass is strange. When glass is very hot, it starts to get red and very soft. As it gets hotter, it starts to melt, just like a candy bar melts on a hot day.

Bottles are made from hot melted glass. The glass goes into a mold that is the shape of the bottle. Then air is blown inside to push the glass against the sides of the mold. When the hot glass cools, there is a bottle inside the mold.

1. What are bottles made from?

2. What happens to glass when it gets very hot?

3. To make a bottle, hot glass goes into a ▓▓▓▓▓▓.

4. When the glass cools, what is left inside the mold?

Owen, Fizz, and Liz
Part Two

A giant named Owen found a little green bottle. He wanted to keep it, but then he started to think about what his mother had told him.

At last, he said to himself, "I think I will send a note to somebody." So he got some paper and tore off a tiny corner. Then he made very small letters on the paper.

When he was done, his note said this.
    Hello.
      My name is Owen, and I live on a very small island. There are many small animals on this island. We have tiny tigers and tiny eagles. We also have other birds that are very tiny. Our bugs are so tiny that you can hardly see them. Please write to me if you get this note.

Owen put the note in the bottle and put the bottle in the water. Slowly it moved out to sea—farther and farther. That bottle drifted and drifted for three days. At last it came to the island where the little people lived.

Two of these people were on the beach. They were named Fizz and Liz. They were not full grown, so they were not even one inch tall yet.

They were throwing grains of sand into the water. For them, a grain of sand was the size of a big stone. As they played, they looked around from time to time. They wanted to make sure there were no spiders around.

Suddenly Liz spotted the bottle bobbing in the water. She said, "Look, there's a giant green thing floating out there."

"Let's see what it is," Fizz said. So Fizz and Liz got in their racing boats. They were really peanut shells, and they were just the right size for one person to sit in and paddle around.

Fizz and Liz paddled out to the giant bottle. "There's something inside," Liz said. "Let's see what it is."

More next time.

A boy named Ted liked to think about things. He thought about what made rain fall. He thought about why things roll down hill. One day, his dad told him, "There's a stream that is two miles from here. And that stream is moving very fast."

Ted thought about what his father told him. Then on Sunday, he went to see the stream. He went to see the stream on the next day and the day after that. Then he told his father, "Dad, you are wrong. That stream is not moving very fast. It was in the same place every time I went to see it."

1. What did Ted like to do?

2. His dad told him that there was a stream that moved ▢.

3. Who went to see that stream?

4. Why didn't Ted think the stream moved fast?

5. What moved fast, the stream or the water in the stream?

sion   ew   tion   aw

1. w<u>i</u>nd
2. w<u>i</u>nd
3. l<u>i</u>ve
4. l<u>i</u>ve
5. r<u>ea</u>d
6. r<u>ea</u>d

1. <u>tugg</u>ed
2. <u>rock</u>ing
3. <u>row</u>ing
4. <u>waded</u>
5. <u>paddl</u>ed
6. <u>drift</u>ed

1. wrote
2. burnt
3. logs
4. knew

1. <u>un</u>roll
2. <u>i</u>magine
3. beaut<u>iful</u>
4. <u>beetles</u>

Owen, Fizz, and Liz
Part Three

Fizz and Liz had to move the giant green bottle to the beach. So they put the noses of their racing boats against the side of the bottle and paddled as hard as they could. When the bottle was very close to the shore, five other people waded into the water and helped roll that bottle out of the water and onto the dry sand.

Four little people crawled into the bottle and tugged at the note. It was hard work, but after a long time, they were able to pull the note out and unroll it. Liz said, "That note is as big as my front yard."

After Fizz and Liz read the note, they thought about Owen's island. Fizz said, "That place is very strange."

They didn't know that Owen's island really looked the same as their island. They didn't know that the bugs on Owen's island looked the same as the bugs on their island. They didn't know that Owen was so big that he could hardly see spiders on his island.

Liz said, "Can you imagine a place with tiny birds?"

"No," Fizz said. "All our birds are bigger than a house."

Later that evening, Liz said, "Why don't we write to Owen and tell him about our island?"

So that's what they did. They turned Owen's letter over and made their note on the back. Turning the paper over was a big job. They wrote letters that were the same size as the letters Owen made. Fizz and Liz made those letters with a burnt log.

Here is their note.

Dear Owen,

Our names are Fizz and Liz, and we live on a beautiful island. It is very big, and it has big animals on it. We have big bears and big birds and big bugs. All the bugs on our island are easy to see because they are so big. Some beetles are the same size we are.

The other little people helped put the note in the bottle and put the bottle in the sea. Everybody watched it drift slowly away from their island.

More to come.

Here are some things you may not know about peanuts. Another name for a peanut is a goober. Peanuts are also called goober peas. You read about Goober. What the story didn't tell you is that he grew a lot of peanuts on his farm.

Here's something else you may not know about peanuts. Peanuts are not really nuts. Real nuts grow on nut trees. Peanuts do not grow on trees. Peanuts grow under ground. They are found on the roots of small plants. Peanuts are called nuts because they have shells that make them look like real nuts.

1. What's another name for peanuts?
2. What kind of plant did Goober grow on his farm?
3. Are peanuts real nuts?
4. Real nuts grow on ▇▇▇▇▇.
5. Where do peanuts grow?
6. What makes peanuts look like real nuts?

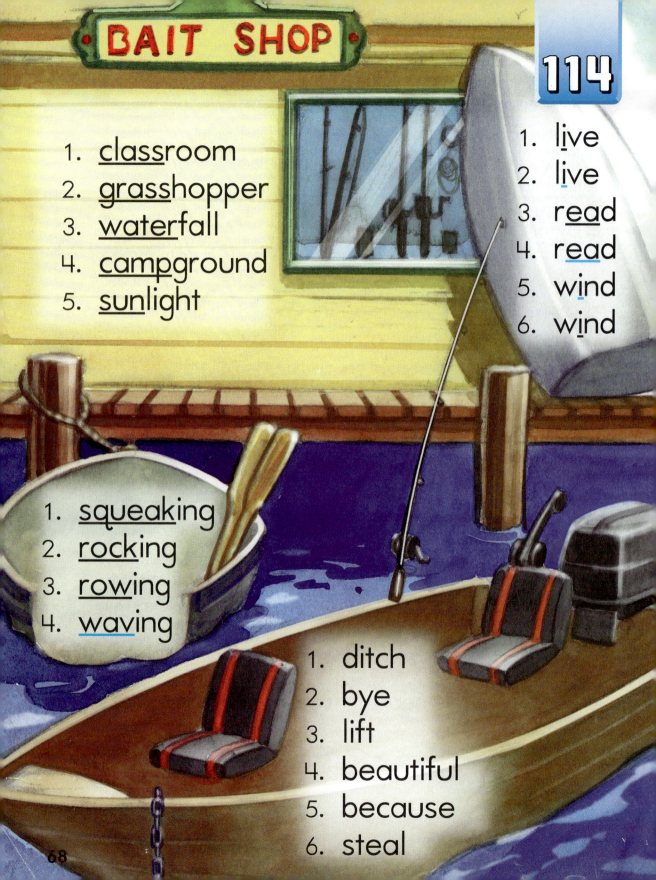

BAIT SHOP — 114

1. <u>class</u>room
2. <u>grass</u>hopper
3. <u>water</u>fall
4. <u>camp</u>ground
5. <u>sun</u>light

1. l<u>i</u>ve
2. l<u>i</u>ve
3. r<u>ea</u>d
4. r<u>ea</u>d
5. w<u>i</u>nd
6. w<u>i</u>nd

1. <u>squeak</u>ing
2. <u>rock</u>ing
3. <u>row</u>ing
4. <u>wav</u>ing

1. ditch
2. bye
3. lift
4. beautiful
5. because
6. steal

Owen, Fizz, and Liz
Part Four

Fizz and Liz sent the green bottle out to sea. Three days later, Owen saw the bottle bobbing up and down in the water. He waded out and picked it up. When he pulled out the note, he said, "Oh, no. That's the same note I sent out."

But just as he was getting ready to throw the note away, he noticed that there was a note on the back. He read it. Then he ran back to his house and read it to his mom and dad. They agreed that Fizz and Liz lived in a strange place. Owen's mom said, "I would hate to live in a place with bugs that were so big."

Then Owen said, "Maybe we should send another note and find out more about their island."

Owen's dad said, "Maybe we should go there and see for ourselves." Owen smiled.

"What?" Owen's mother said. "I wouldn't go to that place. I don't want to see big bugs."

Owen's dad said, "Well, let's think about it."

And they did.

One week later, Owen and his dad said that they wanted to go to the other island.

After two weeks had passed, Owen's mother said that she would go with them.

Their plan was to put the bottle in the water and let it drift. Owen and the others would follow it in their boat. They did not know how long the trip would take, so they loaded their boat with lots of water and food.

As the sun was coming up in the morning, they put the bottle in the water and then followed it in their boat.

"That is our island."

For two days, they were out in the boat with nothing around but water. They did not see any land. They were very tired of sitting in the boat and rocking with the waves.

But on the third day, they spotted land.

Owen's dad started to row toward it. As they came closer and closer to the island, he stopped rowing and said, "Oh, no. That is our island. We must have just drifted out and come back to the place where we started." But he was wrong.

They rowed to the shore and pulled the boat out of the water. Owen's dad said, "Well, let's go home. I'm tired."

More next time.

114

Things drift in water because the water moves. If you look at a river or a stream, you can see the water moving. If you throw a stick in a stream, you can see it move. The water will carry it. When a stream moves, the water is always going down hill. If the water is going down a steep hill, the water moves very fast. If the water is going down a hill that is not steep, the water does not move as fast. If the water goes down a hill that is almost as steep as a wall, the water falls through the air. That's called a waterfall.

1. Things drift in water because ▇▇▇.
    - the water is deep
    - the water is cold
    - the water moves

2. If you throw a stick in a stream, will it move?

3. Does the water in a stream move up hill or down hill?

4. Does it run faster if the hill is very steep or not steep?

5. When water goes down a hill almost as steep as a wall, it's called a ▇▇▇.

1

1. read
2. wind
3. read
4. live
5. wind
6. live

2

1. <u>camp</u>ground
2. <u>waving</u>
3. <u>squeak</u>ing
4. <u>water</u>fall
5. <u>grass</u>hopper

3

1. flood
2. area
3. build
4. building
5. thought
6. through

4

1. idea
2. ditch
3. speck
4. plink
5. dam
6. lifted

Owen, Fizz, and Liz
Part Five

Owen's family thought that they had come back to their island. They were on the beach, on the way to their home. At the same time, Fizz and Liz and five other little people were working on a barn for their turtles and grasshoppers. The turtles could pull big loads. The little people rode their grasshoppers as we would ride horses.

Owen's family walked to where their house would be, but it wasn't there. "What's happening?" his mother said.

"Maybe we are not on our island," Owen said.

Suddenly Owen noticed something that was right where their house would be. It was a tiny barn with only two walls and no roof. When he bent down, he saw something else—tiny, tiny people. Two of these people were waving their tiny arms and making funny squeaking sounds.

Those two people were Fizz and Liz. They knew that one of the giants was Owen because his name was on his shirt. Fizz and Liz were shouting as loud as they could. Those were the funny squeaking sounds.

Owen bent down lower and put his ear right next to them. Then he could hear them saying, "Owen, it is Fizz and Liz."

Owen laughed. The wind from his laugh sent Fizz and Liz sailing into the grass.

So the giants could see why Fizz and Liz talked about bugs that were as big as they were. And Fizz and Liz could see why Owen thought there were tiny bears on his island. Owen and his family went to the beach where they could lay down on the sand. The little people could get close to their ears and talk to them. Of course, Owen and his family could not talk very loudly, or they would blow the little people off the beach. They talked and talked and talked.

Then Owen and his family helped the little people make things. They got sticks and finished the barn. Then they dug a ditch from the waterfall to the farm. Then they dug out an area and made a nice pond and a park next to the farm. Then everybody went to sleep.

More to come.

Toads and Frogs

Toads and frogs lay eggs. When toads and frogs first hatch from their eggs, they are called tadpoles. Tadpoles live in water and don't need air. They look more like fish than frogs or toads. They have a long tail for swimming, but they do not have legs.

Then tadpoles start to change. Their long tails become shorter, and legs start to grow. When tadpoles change completely into frogs or toads, they can not live under water because they need air. But frogs and toads are good swimmers.

Frogs and toads eat a lot of bugs. So farmers like to have frogs and toads around their ponds. Many of the bugs that frogs and toads eat are pests. Some of those bugs bite people, and others eat crops.

1. When frogs and toads first hatch, they are called ▓▓▓▓.
2. They live in ▓▓▓▓.
3. Frogs and toads need ▓▓▓▓ to live.
4. What do frogs eat?
5. Who likes to have frogs and toads around?

116

1. <u>salted</u>
2. <u>campground</u>
3. <u>sun</u>light
4. <u>en</u>joyed
5. <u>lifting</u>

1. scratch
2. speck
3. smoked
4. spoil
5. since

1. wonder
2. water
3. washed
4. watched
5. wander
6. woman

1. flood
2. houses
3. building
4. plink
5. brought

1. eight
2. goodbye
3. idea
4. build

79

Owen, Fizz, and Liz
Part Six

Owen and his family stayed with the little people for three days. In that time, they did more work than the little people could have done in two years. The little people had eight new houses and a beautiful campground near the mountains. They had a large store house for keeping food like fish. And they had lots and lots of fish. Owen and his family had gone fishing and brought back more fish than the little people had ever seen before. After these fish were salted and smoked, Owen's mom put them in the store house.

"How am I going to get my ring?"

The last thing that Owen and his family did was build a dam between the waterfall and the pond they had made. The dam would make sure that the pond would not flood in the spring. Owen and his family had to go part way up the mountain to get rocks for the dam. As Owen's mother was lifting a rock, it slipped. As it fell, it pulled her gold ring off her finger. Plink. The ring fell in a crack between very large rocks. The giants could not reach it with their hands. They could not reach it with a stick. "This is awful," Owen's mom said. "I can't leave without my beautiful ring."

Remember to come visit us.

Suddenly Owen had an idea. He raced down to where the little people were. He picked up Fizz and Liz and raced back. He showed them where the ring was and asked them, "Do you think you could go down there and get the ring?"

"That would be easy," Fizz and Liz said. And it was. In no time, they lifted the ring up so that Owen's mom could get it.

"Oh, thank you," she said.

Then it was time for Owen and his family to go home. They took the green bottle out to the beach and put it in the water. They got into their boat and said goodbye to the little people. The little people waved and shouted. They had tears in their eyes. They stood there and watched the boat and the bottle move out to sea. They could hear the giants calling to them. "So long. Remember to come visit us some time."

At last, the boat was a speck way out in the sea. Fizz and Liz said, "Some day, we will visit Owen's island."

The end.

Differences Between Frogs and Toads

You can see the difference between frog tadpoles and toad tadpoles. Toad tadpoles are darker. Toad tadpoles take longer to grow up. Full grown toads have big bumps on their skin. Most frogs have smooth skin. Toads don't have teeth, but frogs have teeth. Frogs have bigger back legs, so they are able to move more quickly and jump farther.

Frogs and toads eat the same kinds of food. But most frogs hunt for their food when it is day time. Most toads hide during the day and hunt for food at night.

1. Which are darker, toad or frog tadpoles?
2. Which tadpoles grow up faster?
3. What do toads have on their skin that frogs do not have?
4. Frogs have bigger ▬▬▬ ▬▬▬.
5. Toads normally hunt at ▬▬▬.

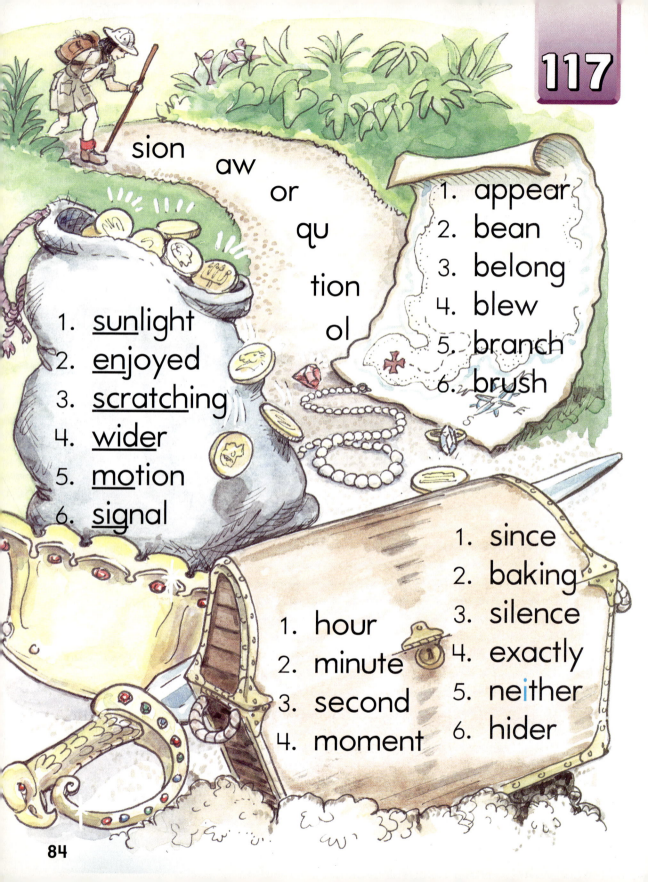

117

sion
aw
or
qu
tion
ol

1. <u>sun</u>light
2. <u>en</u>joyed
3. <u>scratch</u>ing
4. <u>wid</u>er
5. <u>mo</u>tion
6. <u>sig</u>nal

1. appear
2. bean
3. belong
4. blew
5. branch
6. brush

1. hour
2. minute
3. second
4. moment

1. since
2. baking
3. silence
4. exactly
5. neither
6. hider

The Hiding Contest
Part One

A few weeks after the circus, the bragging rats started arguing again. The other rats in the pack were tired of listening to that noisy argument. They went to the wise old rat and said, "We must do something to make Moe and Sherlock shut up. Help us out."

The wise old rat thought for a few minutes and then said, "I think I have a plan that will work."

The wise old rat went over to where Moe and Sherlock were arguing, and he asked, "Which of you rats is the best at hiding?"

Sherlock spoke first. He said that he could hide in the middle of a street in bright sunlight.

Moe spoke next. He said, "I could hide right next to you and you would not be able to see me."

"Stop," the wise old rat said. "There is only one way to settle this argument."

You know how they settled it. They had a hiding contest. The wise old rat told Sherlock and Moe, "You go hide, and after a while, we'll come looking for you. The first one we find is the loser of the contest."

The two rats took off and hid. The wise old rat said to the others, "Now we will have peace for a while. In three hours, we will go looking for them."

One of the other rats said, "I can see them now. Moe is right over there near those weeds, and Sherlock is behind that tree."

The wise old rat said, "I know. But let's enjoy the quiet for a few hours." And that's just what the other rats did. They read and whispered and just enjoyed the peace and quiet.

The time passed pretty slowly for Sherlock and Moe. But for the other rats in the pack, the time seemed to fly. And before they knew it, three hours had passed.

More next time.

There was a baby mouse who loved to bounce her tiny ball. The mouse bounced that ball day and night. One morning, the baby mouse was bouncing the ball, and a cat saw her. That cat whispered to himself, "I will pounce on that mouse."

But just as the cat started to pounce, the tiny ball bounced up and went right in the cat's nose. It was stuck there. The cat started to sneeze, but the ball did not come out.

The mother mouse came out and said, "Ho, ho, Mister Cat. You don't have a mouse in your mouth. You have a ball up your nose."

The ball stayed in the cat's nose for a few hours before it came out. The cat didn't pounce on mice after that.

1. Who loved to bounce her ball?

2. The baby mouse bounced the ball all day and ▓▓▓▓.

3. Who was the cat going to pounce on?

4. The ball got stuck in the cat's ▓▓▓▓.

The Hiding Contest
Part Two

The rat pack enjoyed three hours of silence as the bragging rats hid. At last the wise old rat quietly told the others, "It's time to find Moe and Sherlock. We must find them at exactly the same time."

So some of the rats went over to where Sherlock was behind the tree. He was easy to see because he was scratching and talking to himself. The other rats went over to where Moe was. He was trying to hide behind some weeds in the field, but two crows were right next to him asking what he was doing. When the wise old rat gave the signal, all the other rats said, "We found you."

The wise old rat explained to Sherlock and Moe, "We found both of you at exactly the same time, so neither one of you won the contest."

Moe said, "You found Sherlock first."

Sherlock said, "No way. You found Moe first."

"Stop arguing," the wise old rat said. "We will have to have another hiding contest tomorrow."

"Okay," Moe said. "But tomorrow, I'll hide so well you may never find me."

"Oh yeah?" Sherlock said. "I'm going to hide so well that your children will still be looking for me six years from now."

"Oh yeah?" Moe said. "I'll hide so well that . . ."

The pack had to listen to a lot of arguing that evening. But the next day, they put on another hiding contest. That contest was a lot like the first contest, except that the other rats waited four hours before they found the bragging rats.

And, of course, they found Moe and Sherlock at exactly the same time.

Do you know that those hiding contests are still going on? It's true. Whenever the pack can't stand Sherlock and Moe any longer, they ask them who is the best hider. Then the pack can get Sherlock and Moe to have another hiding contest. For the next few hours, the bragging rats are quiet, and all the other rats are very happy.

The end.

There once was a snake that was sad. The other animals were playing ball. They had legs, so they could kick the ball. The snake did not have legs and could not kick the ball.

One day the snake said, "I think I can hit that ball with my head."

The first time the snake tried to make the ball move by hitting it with its head, the ball did not go very far. But the snake practiced and practiced. At last, the snake could really make that ball move. The snake could even bounce the ball.

The other animals saw the snake hitting the ball with its head and let the snake play ball with them. The snake won the game by hitting the ball very hard. All the other animals said, "That snake really knows how to use its head."

1. At first, why was the snake sad?
2. Why couldn't the snake kick the ball?
3. What did the snake practice hitting the ball with?
4. Did the other animals let the snake play ball?
5. The other animals said, "That snake can really use its ▟▟▟▟."

1. vet
2. oak
3. test
4. heel
5. tip
6. trash

1. s<u>ir</u>
2. ch<u>a</u>rt
3. st<u>ai</u>rs
4. <u>p</u>ainting
5. tr<u>ea</u>t
6. <u>c</u>ouch

1. <u>grate</u>ful
2. <u>after</u>noon
3. <u>glass</u>es
4. <u>holler</u>ing
5. <u>par</u>don
6. <u>hun</u>dreds

1. use
2. rag
3. shave
4. rather
5. scream
6. might

Gorman Gets Glasses

One day, Gorman came into the barn and ran into a pile of pots. Gorman said, "Pardon me, sir. I didn't see you standing there."

Clarabelle said, "Gorman, you're speaking to a pot."

Gorman laughed and said, "I was just making a joke."

"No," Clarabelle said. "You need glasses. The vet is coming to the farm today. I'll bet she can make glasses for you."

So that afternoon, the vet gave Gorman an eye test. She set the chart on a tall oak tree. There were letters on the chart. Gorman stood ten yards from the chart. The vet told him, "Read all the letters. Start with the biggest letter at the top of the chart."

Gorman said, "What chart?"

The vet said, "The chart on the oak tree."

Gorman said, "What oak tree?"

The vet said, "My, my. This goat really needs glasses."

The vet told Gorman to stand closer and closer to the chart. He still couldn't see. Finally he was only one foot from the chart, and he could read the big letter **E** at the top.

The vet said, "I will have glasses for you two weeks from now."

When the vet returned, she put the eye chart in front of the oak tree. She told Gorman to keep his eyes closed as she tied the new glasses around his ears. Then she said, "Open your eyes and tell me what you see."

Gorman looked around and jumped. "Help," he hollered. "What is that great brown and white thing next to me?"

Clarabelle said, "Gorman, that's me."

After Gorman named all the letters on the eye chart, he went to the pond and looked at himself in the water. "Who is that silly looking animal?" he asked.

Just then, his glasses slipped off and fell into the water. Gorman said, "Oh, no. I will never find my glasses now."

A voice said, "Don't say never." Then the voice said, "Brothers, sisters, and pals, let's see who can find those glasses."

Within seconds, hundreds of toads were in the pond. They found Gorman's glasses, and Gorman was very grateful, of course. After he put on his glasses, he told the leader toad, "You are a strange looking animal, but I would like to be your friend." And that's just what happened.

The end.

Once there was a tom cat that lived in the city, but he didn't have a home. One night was very cold. All the other cats were complaining because they didn't have anything warm to sleep on. The tom cat said, "I'll show you how to get some things."

He got up on a fence and started to howl very loudly. "Meoooooowwwww," he howled.

Some other cats joined in and started howling, too. Within a few seconds, people started to throw things at the cats. Somebody threw a big shoe. Somebody else threw an old rug. Somebody else threw a coat with a hole in it.

The tom cat said, "Now we have lots of good things to sleep on."

The cats made a pile out of the things, and even though the night was very cold, the cats were warm. They had a good sleep.

1. Did the tom cat have a home?

2. What kind of night was it?
   - warm   • cold   • hot

3. Write three things that people threw at the cats.

4. Were the cats warm that night?

121

1. l<u>ea</u>sh
2. cha<u>nce</u>
3. tra<u>sh</u>
4. c<u>o</u>uch

1. <u>y</u>esterday
2. <u>locki</u>ng
3. <u>you</u>'ve
4. <u>scratched</u>
5. t<u>i</u>pping

1. Noser
2. taught
3. office
4. mitten

1. coll<u>ar</u>
2. checked
3. heel
4. treat
5. use
6. gate

Noser
Part One

Noser was a dog that had a great nose. He lived with a family of five people, but his best pal in that family was Pam. She fed him and played with him. She went walking with him. And she taught him some tricks. She taught him to sit, to shake hands, to come when she called him, and to heel. When a dog heels, the dog walks right next to you.

Noser's nose was so good that he could find anything. Sometimes Pam would take a little dog treat and hide it in the living room. She'd tell Noser, "Go find your treat." No matter where she hid it, he'd find it in a few seconds. One time, she put a treat under the seat of the couch. Then she sat on the couch. That didn't make any difference. In a few seconds, Noser was trying to push her out of the way so he could get the treat.

One time, Pam bet one of her pals that she could hide her mittens anywhere in the yard and Noser would find them in less than a minute. Pam won the bet. It took Noser less than ten seconds to find the mittens.

Noser had one problem with his nose. He loved to use it. He could use his nose a little bit when he stayed at home. But when he went out, he could really use his nose. So he loved to get out and go sniffing. There were new things to find, new dogs to meet, new cats and rabbits to chase, and new trash cans to sniff.

That was one of the things Noser loved best—sniffing trash cans. Noser's nose told him if a trash can had some good things to eat inside. If it did, he'd try to tip it over and get the lid off. If people didn't finish all of their dinner, and put it in their trash can, Noser would finish that dinner for them. He might have to make a big mess before he got to the food, but if it was in the trash can, Noser would find it.

Trash cans were not the only things Noser sniffed. Sometimes people put dog food out for their dog. Sometimes their dog would not eat it before Noser came sniffing around. If Noser found it, Noser would eat it. He'd also eat cat food if he found it. In fact, he liked cat food more than dog food.

But what Noser liked most about getting out and sniffing around was that he was free. He could run here or there, and just go where his nose took him. If he got very far from home, he could find his way back with no more trouble than you have finding your way across a room. He would just use his wonderful nose.

More next time.

121

One time a cow named Clarabelle wanted to be like a mole. She saw moles dig holes in the ground. She said, "I would like to dig a big hole for me."

So she got up the next morning and went out to the middle of the field. She said, "This is a good place to start digging." And she did. Her legs were not good for digging, but she stamped and kicked and started to make dirt fly this way and that way. By noon, she had a very deep hole. And she was down in that hole. The other animals watched her dig down deeper and deeper. Soon they could not see Clarabelle anymore.

1. What animal did Clarabelle want to be like?
2. What did she want to do?
3. Were her legs good for digging?
4. Did she dig a deep hole?
5. Could the other animals see Clarabelle in her deep hole?

1. <u>fl</u>uffy
2. <u>y</u>ou've
3. <u>scr</u>atched
4. <u>ch</u>ecked

1. hop
2. hope
3. hoping
4. hopping

1. office
2. taught
3. collar
4. yesterday
5. knew
6. raced

1. change
2. chance
3. leash
4. locked
5. gate

Noser
Part Two

Noser had a problem. The things that he loved to do were not the things that Pam wanted him to do. She wanted him to stay in the yard or stay on a leash. He wanted to run after his nose. The only way he could do that was to run away. He didn't like to run away, because he knew that Pam didn't want him to. But the only way he could find good things to sniff was to run away. So every chance he had, he would sneak out of the house or sneak out of the back yard.

Pam tried to keep him on a leash or keep him in the yard. But Noser would get away at least one time every week. He'd always come back. But that could be the next day.

Each time Noser ran away, Pam would find out about the things he did. Maybe the people who lived next door would tell Pam that Noser ate their cat's dinner. Maybe a person on the next block would tell her that Noser knocked over their trash can and made a great mess in their yard. Maybe someone would call Pam to tell her that Noser had chased their cat up a tree.

Pam didn't like these calls. And she tried to make sure that Noser didn't get out of the yard. She kept him on a leash when she walked with him, and she was careful about locking the gate to the yard. But Noser still got away a lot. He would dig under the fence, and sometimes he would sneak out of the house when somebody was coming in.

One day, Pam's mom told her, "If Noser keeps getting away, we're going to have to get rid of him."

"No, Mom," Pam said. "We can't do that."

That afternoon, Pam had a long talk with Noser. She took him to her room. She told him that she loved him and didn't want to lose him. She said, "But you can't keep digging under the fence and sneaking away. You've got to stay in the yard."

Noser scratched his ear and yawned. Pam said, "Oh Noser, you're not listening to a thing I'm saying." Noser yawned again.

Later that day, Pam took Noser for a walk. He wanted to sniff for rabbits and cats, but she told him to heel, and he followed her order. When she got back to her house, she opened the gate and put Noser in the yard. She took off the leash and started to close the gate.

Before she knew what happened, Noser sneaked out through the gate and then ran away, very fast. "Noser," she called. "Noser, come back here." But Noser was running along, sniffing the air and not thinking much about what Pam was saying.

More to come.

122

Clarabelle wanted to be like a mole, so she dug a great big hole. That hole was so deep that the other animals could not even see her any more. Clarabelle liked the hole she had dug, but after a while she said, "I need to get out of this hole and eat some grass." So she tried to get out of the hole. But she couldn't. The hole was so deep that she just slipped around when she tried to get out. She called to the other animals. "Help me," she said. "I need to get out of this hole."

The other animals looked at each other and said, "What can we do to get her out of that hole?" Then they said, "We don't know what to do."

1. Clarabelle wanted to be like a ▇▇▇▇▇.
2. Why did she want to get out of her hole?
3. Was she able to get out of the hole?
4. Who did she call to?
5. Did the other animals know how to get her out of the hole?

Noser
Part Three

When Pam told her mom and dad that Noser got away, her mom said, "Well, he'd better not get in any trouble. If he does, we're going to have to get rid of him."

"Mom," Pam said. "Don't blame him. I'm the one you should blame. I wasn't careful around the gate, and he got out."

Her mom said, "Honey, it doesn't matter. He's done this a hundred times before. We can't let it keep going on."

Noser didn't come home that night. Pam walked around the streets near her house and called for him, but she didn't find him. Pam checked all around the house before she went to bed, but she didn't see Noser.

Noser did not show up the next morning. Pam's mom said, "I'll wait until noon before I call the dog pound."

Pam went to school a little later than she did on other days. She wanted to stay at home as long as she could. She kept hoping that Noser would come home, but he didn't. She ran to school so she wouldn't be late.

Just as she was going in the front door, she saw a dog sitting in the hall. It was Noser. Some kids were petting him. He smelled bad. That smell told Pam that he'd been tipping over trash cans.

She grabbed him by the collar and took him to the office. She called her mom and said, "I found Noser. He's in school. Could you pick him up and take him home?"

"Yes," her mom said. But she didn't sound very happy.

Pam said, "And he stinks."

When Pam got home after school, Noser was in the back yard, wagging his tail. He was clean and didn't smell bad anymore. Pam knew that her mom had given him a bath. Pam told the dog, "Noser, you've got to stop running away."

Pam went inside. A woman was talking to Pam's mom in the kitchen. The woman was saying, "So I had to find a ladder and climb up the tree to get Fluffy down. She was so scared that she scratched me." The woman showed scratch marks on her hands.

Pam's mom said, "I'm very sorry. We try to be careful, but Noser got away yesterday."

The woman said, "And that's not all. I had to spend almost an hour cleaning up trash in my back yard. Your dog went digging in my cans and left trash all over the place."

Pam's mom said, "Well, all I can say is that I'm very sorry, and it won't happen again."

More to come.

Clarabelle was stuck in the hole she had dug. The other animals did not know how to get her out. A pig said, "I have a plan. Let's go get a ladder and put it in the hole. Then Clarabelle could use the ladder to get out."

The animals tried that plan. They got a ladder from the barn and put it in the hole. But when Clarabelle tried to go up the ladder, it broke, and she fell back in the hole.

Clarabelle was very unhappy. She said, "I need to get out so I can eat."

1. Where was Clarabelle?
2. What kind of animal had a plan to get her out?
3. What did the animals put into the hole?
4. Did the plan work?
5. Clarabelle needed to get out so she could _____.

1. <u>m</u>a<u>m</u>a
2. <u>a</u>n<u>g</u>ry
3. <u>fl</u>a<u>sh</u>light
4. <u>dr</u>i<u>v</u>eway

1. <u>D</u>i<u>ck</u>
2. poli<u>ce</u>
3. offi<u>ce</u>r
4. <u>c</u>o<u>u</u>nt

1. <u>h</u>ero
2. <u>b</u>aby
3. <u>be</u>longs
4. <u>fo</u>rever

1. raccoon
2. gone
3. shoe
4. uncle
5. rushed
6. picture

1. touch
2. shovel
3. hugs
4. worry

Noser
Part Four

A woman was telling about the things Noser did in her yard. Pam's mom looked very angry.

Pam said to the woman, "If it does happen again, you could call me. I'd get your cat down from the tree, and I'd clean up the mess."

"No," Pam's mom said. "It won't happen again."

After the woman left, Pam's mom said, "Pam, I called your Uncle Dick and told him about Noser. He said he would let Noser live with him on the farm."

"For how long?" Pam asked.

"Forever," her mom said.

"No, Mom. Please. Give him one more chance."

"Sorry, honey. He's had his last chance."

124

Pam ran to her room and cried. At dinner, she tried to talk to her mom about keeping Noser, but her mom didn't change her mind.

Pam was sad that evening. She put a leash on Noser and took him for a walk. She was thinking that it might be her last walk with Noser.

Pam and Noser were three blocks from home when Pam saw a lot of police cars and people in front of a brown house. When she got closer, she asked a police officer, "Why are all these people around here?"

He said, "The baby girl who lives here is missing. Her mom was playing with her in the back yard. The mother went inside to answer the phone. When she went back to the yard, she found that the wind had blown the gate open. The baby was gone."

The police officer held up a little shoe. "This is the only thing she could find, one of the baby's shoes."

Pam thought for a moment and then said, "Maybe Noser can find her. Noser can find anything."

"Well . . . . " the police officer said and scratched his head. He looked around and then said, "I don't see how that would do any harm."

Pam said, "Hand me that shoe. I'll let Noser sniff it."

The police officer handed the shoe to Pam, and she held it in front of Noser. "Noser, this belongs to a baby . . . baby. Smell the baby's shoe."

Noser could tell from the way Pam was talking that she wanted him to find something. He wagged his tail. He sniffed the shoe she was holding. Then he sniffed the police officer's leg.

Pam tried to show Noser that he should think about the shoe, but he didn't seem to understand what she wanted.

More to come.

124

Clarabelle was in the hole she had dug. She told the other animals that she needed to eat. So the other animals got a lot of grass and dropped it into the hole. Clarabelle ate the grass and thanked the other animals. But she still wanted to get out of the hole. A sheep said, "Let's drop a long rope in the hole. Then we could pull Clarabelle out of the hole." So the animals got a rope from the barn and dropped one end in the hole. Clarabelle held onto that end. The other animals pulled and pulled as hard as they could pull. But they could not pull Clarabelle out of the hole.

1. Who needed to eat?
2. What did the other animals drop into the hole for her to eat?
3. What kind of animal had a new plan to get her out of the hole?
4. What did the animals drop into the hole?
5. Were the other animals able to pull Clarabelle out?

1. touch**ed**
2. point**ed**
3. hug**ged**
4. answer**ed**

1. police
2. raccoon
3. mama
4. worry
5. hero
6. stack

1. **flash**light
2. **drive**way
3. **week**end
4. **door**bell
5. **Sun**day
6. **news**paper

1. d**u**ring
2. Sat**u**rday
3. **sh**ined
4. **sh**ovel

Noser
Part Five

Pam was trying to get Noser to look for a lost baby, but Noser did not seem to know what she wanted him to do. She asked the police officer, "Can we go to the last place where the baby was in the yard?"

There were a lot of people in the yard, and Noser had a lot of things to sniff. The police officer led Pam and Noser to a place near the gate. "Here's where the baby was," the police officer said.

Pam put the shoe on the ground. "Noser," she said and touched the ground next to the shoe. "Baby. Go find baby." Noser sniffed the ground. Then Pam pulled Noser toward the gate. She pointed to the ground again. "Baby. Find baby." Noser sniffed the ground.

She led Noser through the gate, and Noser started sniffing. "I think he's trying now," Pam said to the police officer. Some other people were watching Noser as he pulled Pam along.

Noser led Pam and the others to a house near the corner. Then Noser went to a small hole under the house and sniffed. He scratched at the hole. The police officer shined his flashlight in the hole and said, "There's nothing in there. He must be on a trail of a raccoon."

After a little while, the police officer and the others started walking back to the brown house.

Pam tried to pull Noser away from the hole, but he wouldn't move. Then Pam heard a tiny voice say "Mama" and start to cry.

"Officer," Pam shouted. "The baby is here. Noser found her."

Everybody rushed back to the hole. When they listened, they could hear the tiny voice of the baby. The hole was too small for any of the people to get in. But a few minutes later, some people ran up with shovels and digging bars. They made the hole bigger. Then a boy was able to crawl through the hole and go under the house. He found the baby behind a stack of old newspapers.

When the police officer pulled the baby out of the hole, people cheered. The baby's mother cried. She hugged her baby and patted Noser. "Oh, thank you for saving my baby," she said.

Before Pam knew what was happening, people were asking her questions and taking pictures of her and Noser. Pam answered questions and more questions. After a while, she said, "I have to get home. My mom will worry about me."

The police officer patted Noser and told Pam, "You should be very proud to have a dog like that. He's a real hero."

More to come.

Clarabelle was in the hole she had dug. "I want to go home," she cried. "I don't want to be like a mole."

The other animals talked and argued about how to get Clarabelle out of the hole. At last the leader toad jumped up on Gorman's head and said, "Fill the hole with water. Clarabelle will swim to the top, and we'll pull her out."

The other animals liked the plan. So they dumped buckets and buckets of water into the hole. As the hole filled up, Clarabelle swam around. At last, she came to the top and the other animals pulled her out. Clarabelle thanked the other animals and gave the leader toad a big wet kiss.

1. Which animal had a new plan to get Clarabelle out of the hole?
2. What did the animals put in the hole?
3. As the hole filled up, what did Clarabelle do?
   - dug
   - swam
   - cried
4. Did Clarabelle come to the top of the hole?
5. Who pulled her out of the hole?
6. Who did Clarabelle kiss?

1. <u>d</u>i<u>e</u>d
2. <u>glow</u>ed
3. <u>own</u>ed
4. <u>friend</u>s
5. <u>bang</u>ed

1. <u>newsp</u>aper
2. <u>week</u>end
3. <u>Sun</u>day
4. <u>door</u>bell

1. <u>Satur</u>day
2. <u>must</u>ard
3. <u>back</u>ward
4. <u>kit</u>chen

1. mirror
2. during
3. might
4. fight
5. strong
6. curled

Noser
Part Six

The morning newspaper had a big story about Noser. It also had pictures of him next to the baby. The paper called Noser a hero. The paper also said that if Noser hadn't found the baby, the baby could have died. The police officer had told the newspaper, "You could hardly hear the baby's voice because she was behind a pile of newspapers. The people who owned the house were out of town, so nobody would have been able to hear the baby."

Everybody at school knew about Noser and what he had done. The police officer even came to Pam's classroom and told everybody the story about how Noser found the baby.

Pam was very happy and proud. But she was also sad because she knew that Noser was going to have to live with Uncle Dick.

When she got home from school, she saw Uncle Dick's truck in the driveway. He was inside talking to Pam's mom. He gave Pam a hug and said, "Well, I can't take your dog now. He's a hero. But here's what I can do. Every weekend I'll pick him up and take him to my place. I'll let him run and sniff all he wants. Then I'll bring him back every Sunday evening."

Pam gave him a hug and said, "Could I go with Noser some times?"

"Sure," he said. "Come out and spend a day or spend all weekend. We'll have a good time."

Pam asked her mother, "Could we do that? Could we keep Noser?"

Her mom shook her head, "I don't know. The people who live around here don't like him, and . . ."

"Oh, please, Mom," Pam said.

Just then the doorbell rang. The woman who owned the cat Fluffy was at the door. She was with two other people who lived near Pam. The woman who owned Fluffy said, "We have all been here before to tell about the bad things Noser did. We're here this time to tell you that we think Noser did a wonderful thing, and we want him to stay around here."

Pam's mom said, "Well, thank you so much. But he might get out again. He's . . ."

Pam said, "But if he does, just call me. I'll come over and take care of the mess." Everybody thought that was a good plan.

So Noser still lives with Pam during the week. Once in a while, he gets out and goes sniffing, and sometimes people get pretty mad at him. But even when they are mad at him, they are still proud to have a hero dog live near them.

On some weekends, Pam goes with Noser to Uncle Dick's place. She runs through the fields and the forests with Noser, and they have a very good time.

The end.

126

Marvin was an eagle. But Marvin did not like to fly, because he always bumped into things. Marvin's sister was good at flying. She didn't bump into anything when she went flying. And each time Marvin bumped into something, his sister said the same thing. "My, my, Marvin can't fly. Why can't Marvin stay in the sky?"

That made Marvin mad. But Marvin still bumped into things every time he tried to fly. One day Marvin made up his mind that he would fly without bumping into something. He told his sister. "I can fly. I can fly. I can stay up in the sky." But when Marvin took off, he went flying right into the barn. You know what his sister said.

1. Did Marvin like to fly?
2. What happened each time he tried to fly?
3. Who was better at flying, Marvin or his sister?
4. Each time Marvin bumped into something, his sister said, "Why can't Marvin stay in ▇▇▇?"
5. Did Marvin make up his mind to fly better?
6. What did he fly into at the end of this part?

127

dis

1. believe
2. disbelieve
3. appear
4. disappear
5. agree
6. disagree

1. <u>c</u>oun<u>t</u>er
2. <u>sl</u>i<u>pp</u>er
3. <u>f</u>i<u>ght</u>er
4. <u>gl</u>ow<u>ing</u>

1. snack
2. stack
3. beam
4. press
5. jar
6. glass

1. s<u>qu</u>i<u>r</u>t
2. mustard
3. empty
4. burning

Sweetie and the Mirror

One day the woman who owned Sweetie took him to a friend's house. Sweetie had never been there before. At first, he just sat in the kitchen. Then he thought he would look around, so he went into the other rooms.

Suddenly he saw something he had never seen before. It was a mirror. That mirror was on a door, and it went all the way to the floor.

Sweetie did not know that it was a mirror. To him, it looked like another part of the room. But as Sweetie moved in front of the mirror, he suddenly saw something that made him very mad. He saw another cat in front of him.

He said to himself, "What is that ugly cat doing here?"

Then he thought, "I'll show that cat how mean and strong I am." So Sweetie made a mean face. But the other yellow cat made a mean face at the same time Sweetie did.

Sweetie showed his teeth, and the other cat did the same thing. Sweetie held up a paw and showed his long, sharp claws to the other cat. But the other cat showed his claws to Sweetie at the same time. Sweetie said to himself, "That cat may be ugly, but it has to be the fastest cat I have ever seen. As soon as I do something, that cat does it at the same time."

Then Sweetie said, "I know how to scare this cat. I will leap at him."

So Sweetie got close to the floor. He got his legs ready for a big leap, and then he jumped as hard as he could. He went flying through the air. Bonk. He banged his head against the mirror and bounced backward. He landed on his back on the floor. He rolled around. And finally he looked at the cat in the mirror. That cat was looking at Sweetie.

Sweetie said to himself, "That cat may be ugly, but that cat is fast, and it can really hit hard."

The next time Sweetie's owner took him to the house with the ugly yellow cat, Sweetie just curled up under the table in the kitchen and stayed there. He never found out who that yellow cat was.

The end.

Marvin had tried to fly, and he went flying right into the barn. Bang. His sister smiled and said, "My, my, Marvin can't fly. Why can't Marvin stay in the sky?"

The next day, Marvin tried again. He took off and started flying right at the barn. Did he bump into the barn? No. He flew right over the barn. Marvin shouted to his sister, "I can fly. I can fly. I can stay up in the sky."

A few seconds later, he flew right into a tree. You know what his sister said.

Marvin was very sad. He went home. Did he fly home? No. He walked home.

1. What did Marvin fly into in the last part?
2. Did Marvin try to fly again in this part?
3. When he took off, he started flying right toward ▊▊▊.
4. Did he fly into the barn?
5. When he was in the air, he told his sister, "I can stay up in ▊▊▊."
6. But then he flew into a ▊▊▊.
7. How did he get home?

1. dis<u>join</u>
2. dis<u>orderly</u>
3. dis<u>appear</u>
4. dis<u>agree</u>
5. dis<u>believe</u>

1. <u>jars</u>
2. <u>squirt</u>ed
3. <u>counter</u>
4. <u>glow</u>ing
5. <u>grow</u>ing
6. <u>fight</u>ers
7. <u>burn</u>t

1. quart<u>er</u>
2. thous<u>and</u>
3. cov<u>er</u>
4. stubb<u>y</u>
5. out<u>er</u>
6. pre<u>ss</u>

1. space
2. empty
3. smelled
4. smiled
5. snack
6. beam

The Mustard Jar

This is a story about a mustard jar that came to life.

Before that happened, the mustard jar looked like hundreds of other mustard jars. It was made of glass, and it was full of yellow mustard. To make the mustard squirt out, you would press on the top of the jar.

The mustard jar came to life when two people from outer space had a fight in the snack bar where the mustard jar was. The mustard jar was on the counter of this snack bar. A small space person was hiding behind the counter. The other space person shot a strange beam of green light at her. That beam missed her, but it hit the mustard jar. And that's what made the mustard jar come to life.

At first, the mustard jar glowed. While it was glowing, the fight kept going on between the space people. A beam of green light hit the wall and started a little fire. Another beam hit the floor and started a fire. A third beam hit the small space person.

A moment later, both the space people disappeared, and the snack bar was empty except for the mustard jar. It was still glowing, but it was also growing.

Somebody called the fire station, and soon a fire truck pulled up outside. The fire fighters ran into the snack bar and put out the fires. Then one of them saw the glowing mustard jar on the counter. By now the mustard jar was as big as a large sack. The fire fighter said, "Look at this great big mustard jar. I think it's getting bigger and bigger."

The other fire fighters stared at the mustard jar. Then they called some experts and told the experts that they had found a mustard jar that was glowing and growing.

By the time the experts got to the snack bar, the mustard jar was as tall as a chair. The experts felt it, smelled it, put their ears next to it, and stared at it for a long time. They agreed, "We have never seen anything like this."

The experts put the mustard jar in a truck and took it to a place where they could find out more about it. By the time they got to this place, the mustard jar was as tall as most women. When they tried to lift it out of the truck, the mustard jar suddenly moved, and the experts jumped back. One expert said, "It can move."

A voice said, "And I can talk."

The experts jumped back again. One of them asked, "Did that mustard jar talk?"

The mustard jar said, "Yes, I can talk because I can be just like you."

More next time.

The next day Marvin tried to fly again. He took off and flew over the barn. Then he flew over the tree. He shouted to his sister, "I can fly. I can fly. I can stay up in the sky."

Marvin was so happy that he started to fly faster and faster.

But when he was going very, very fast, he flew right into the side of a big cow. Marvin was going so fast when he hit the cow that the cow almost fell down. Marvin's sister laughed and laughed. She said, "My, my, Marvin can't fly. Why can't Marvin stay in the sky?"

The cow looked very mad. Marvin said, "I'm sorry. I'm sorry."

1. In this part of the story, did Marvin fly into the barn?
2. Did Marvin fly into the tree?
3. Marvin was so happy that he started to fly very ▇▇▇▇.
4. What did he run into?
5. Did the cow look happy or mad?
6. Who said, "My, my, Marvin can't fly"?
7. Who said, "I'm sorry"?

re

129

1. reorder
2. rejoin
3. reheat
4. refill

1. squirting
2. quarter
3. thousand
4. love
5. glove

1. chief
2. glop
3. covered
4. burnt
5. slip
6. slipper
7. slippery

1. sleeve
2. hire
3. hose
4. helmet
5. boots
6. streak

The Mustard Jar Gets Arms and Legs

The mustard jar had grown until it was as big as most women. The jar said, "I can make myself be just like you and do anything you can do."

One expert said, "We can smile, but how can you smile? You don't even have a mouth."

The mustard jar said, "I can make a mouth. Watch." A little line appeared in the glass, and the line seemed to smile.

Another expert said, "We can walk, but you don't even have legs."

"Watch this," the mustard jar said, and little stubby yellow legs appeared at the bottom of the jar. They looked pretty silly, and one of the experts started to laugh.

"Why are you laughing?" the mustard jar asked.

The expert said, "Well, your legs are a little funny."

"They are not," said the mustard jar, and shot a great glop of mustard at the expert who was laughing. It covered his shirt.

"Ugh," he said.

The mustard jar said, "Does anybody else think my legs are funny?"

The other experts said, "No. Those are fine legs."

The mustard jar said, "And if I need arms, I can have arms. Watch." Two little stubby yellow arms appeared at the side of the great big mustard jar. The mustard jar did not look like a person with arms and legs. It looked like a great big mustard jar with little stubby arms and legs.

The experts tried not to laugh, but one of them could not hold back.

As soon as she started laughing, a great glop of yellow mustard shot out and landed on her shirt. She stopped laughing and complained, "You have no right to . . ."

Another great glop of yellow mustard shot out and went right in her mouth.

The experts didn't laugh at the mustard jar after that happened. But they talked with the mustard jar for a long time. One of the experts asked the mustard jar, "What kinds of things would you like to do?"

The mustard jar said, "I would like to have a job."

"What kind of job would you like?"

The mustard jar thought for a moment and then said, "I think I would like to be a fire fighter. I saw some of them at the snack bar, and I think fire fighting would be a good job for me."

The experts said, "Well, let's see if we can get you a job as a fire fighter."

More to come.

What kind of job would you like?

129

Marvin went flying right into the side of a big cow. That cow looked mad. But the cow was not mad at Marvin. The cow was mad at Marvin's sister. The cow said to her, "Don't make fun of Marvin. He helped me by running into me. I had a mean bug in my ear. When Marvin ran into me, the bug popped out of my ear. Thank you, Marvin."

So Marvin and the cow became good pals. Marvin's sister stopped making fun of him. And Marvin became very good at flying. He flies with his sister, and they say, "We can fly. We can fly. We can stay up in the sky."

1. Was the cow mad at Marvin or at Marvin's sister?
2. What was in the cow's ear?
3. What popped out of the ear when Marvin hit the cow?
4. The cow told Marvin's sister not to ■■■■.
5. Can Marvin fly well now?
6. Who is Marvin's pal?

131

1. plane
2. chief
3. helmet
4. boots
5. sleeves
6. hose

1. retell
2. reprint
3. replay
4. recharge

1. sidewalk
2. hallway
3. itself
4. hillside

1. allow
2. city
3. hire
4. higher
5. gloves
6. slippery

The Mustard Jar Fights Fires

The experts told the mustard jar that they would try to get it a job as a fire fighter. When the experts brought the mustard jar to the fire station, the fire fighters could not believe what they saw. "Is that really a mustard jar?" they asked each other.

The mustard jar smiled and told the fire fighters, "I can be a fire fighter, just like the rest of you."

One fire fighter said, "If you're a fire fighter, you have to wear a coat, a helmet, gloves, and boots."

The mustard jar said, "That sounds good to me."

But they couldn't find things that fit the mustard jar. The boots were too tall for those stubby little legs, and the coat sleeves were too long for those stubby little arms.

When the mustard jar tried on the biggest coat in the fire station, a fire fighter named Sam started laughing.

A great glop of yellow mustard shot out from the mustard jar and hit Sam right in the face. None of the other fire fighters laughed at the mustard jar after that happened.

The experts told the mustard jar, "We will hire somebody to make things that fit you." And they did that.

Two days later, the mustard jar had a new coat, a helmet, gloves, and boots. Just as it was trying them on, the alarm sounded, and all the fire fighters rushed to get on the fire truck. That truck roared down the street to the fire.

An old store was in flames. The chief of the fire fighters told the mustard jar to take the fire hose up the ladder and squirt water on the building. The mustard jar couldn't climb the ladder because its legs were too short.

And the jar couldn't hang onto the hose because its arms were too short. After the jar dropped the hose three times, the chief told the mustard jar, "Go sit in the truck. I'll take care of the fire hose."

The mustard jar was very sad, but it went to the truck. Just as it was getting in, a fire fighter came running out of the store. "Chief," she shouted. "Sam is trapped inside. He's in the hall, but he's stuck. I can't get him out."

The mustard jar ran into the burning building, squirting mustard this way and that way. Great piles of mustard put out a lot of the fires in the hall. Now the mustard jar could see Sam through the smoke. His leg was stuck in a hole in the floor. "I'm stuck," Sam said.

The mustard jar said, "I can make your leg slippery." The mustard jar squirted a great glop of mustard on Sam's leg. The mustard made the leg so slippery that it slid right out of the hole.

More to come.

131

Zelda was an artist. But Zelda didn't always draw what she should have drawn. One time, Mrs. Hudson wrote a story about the wonderful time she had on the Snake River. The story told about how they went down the river in a raft. Here is part of what she wrote. "Our raft floated down the river. It was yellow with red stripes."

Zelda's painting did not show what Mrs. Hudson wanted.

1. Who wrote the story?
2. Who made the pictures for the story?
3. What did Mrs. Hudson want to be yellow with red stripes?
4. What did Zelda make yellow with red stripes?

A
1. revisit
2. resend
3. disappear
4. discharge

B
1. <u>up</u>set
2. <u>hall</u>way
3. <u>side</u>walk
4. <u>out</u>fit
5. <u>air</u>plane
6. <u>hand</u>cuffs

C
1. booth
2. moan
3. key
4. gas
5. crowd
6. shower

D
1. plunger
2. station
3. ugly
4. amazing
5. city
6. allowed

A New Job for the Mustard Jar

The mustard jar and Sam were in a hallway, and there were still fires near them. Sam said, "Let's get out of here fast." So Sam and the mustard jar ran down the hall as fast as they could. When Sam got to the place where there were deep piles of slippery mustard, Sam's feet went out from under him, and he went down on his seat.

Sam slid down the hall, through the front door, and out into the street.

Sam's seat was covered with mustard, and he left an ugly yellow streak across the sidewalk. The mustard jar was sliding right behind Sam. When Sam tried to stand up, the mustard jar slid into him, and Sam slid right into the chief, leaving another ugly yellow streak across the street.

When Sam hit the chief, the chief fell on top of Sam, who was covered with mustard. Of course, the chief got covered with mustard.

The people who were watching the fire started to laugh. The mustard jar said, "It's not nice to laugh at fire fighters." A moment later, large glops of mustard squirted into the crowd. Nobody laughed after that happened.

The next day, there were pictures of the fire in the newspaper. One picture showed the chief and Sam standing next to the mustard jar. Everybody was covered with mustard. The story in the paper said, "Amazing mustard jar saves fire fighter and helps put out fire with thousands of pounds of mustard."

Not everybody was happy about the mustard jar being a fire fighter. The people who got squirted by the mustard jar complained.

They wrote a lot of letters. They said that the mustard jar should not be allowed to work as a fire fighter.

Too many people want you to leave the city.

Two days later, the chief told the mustard jar, "I would like to keep you here, but there have been too many people complaining. You won't be able to work in this city."

"But I want to be a fire fighter," the mustard jar said.

The chief told the jar, "Well, there's a little town near here that needs a fire fighter. I'll see what I can do. Maybe I can get you a job there."

Two days later, the mustard jar was on the way to the little town of Big Stone. The mustard jar was ready to be their new fire fighter, but the mustard jar never reached the fire station.

More next time.

132

Zelda made pictures for other parts of the story that Mrs. Hudson wrote about the Snake River. Zelda made a very funny picture for one part of the story. But Zelda did not know that the picture was funny. She thought that it showed just what Mrs. Hudson wrote in her story. Here's what she wrote.

"We spent our first night camping near the river. We had to put up a large tent. Mr. Willis did most of the work while we rested. Our camp chairs were near the tent stakes. Mr. Willis hammered them into the ground."

1. Zelda made pictures for a story about the ▇▇▇▇▇ River.
2. Who wrote this story?
3. Where were the camp chairs?
4. Who hammered something?
5. In Zelda's picture, what did Mr. Willis hammer into the ground?
6. Is that the picture that Mrs. Hudson wanted?

The Mustard Jar Goes to Jail

The mustard jar never made it to the fire station in the little town of Big Stone because police put it in jail.

Here's what happened. The mustard jar remembered to bring its coat, its helmet, and its boots to Big Stone. But the jar forgot its gloves. So as soon as it got to Big Stone, the jar stopped at a phone booth next to a gas station. The jar wanted to tell the chief about the gloves.

The jar put in one quarter, but the call didn't go through. The jar put in another quarter, but the call still didn't go through. The jar didn't have any more quarters. So the jar went to the gas station.

The owner was inside. So were two men dressed in clown outfits. At first the mustard jar didn't know what the clowns were doing, but then the jar saw that they were robbing the gas station.

When the owner saw the mustard jar come in, he said, "Oh, no. There are three robbers. Two of them are clowns, and one is a mustard jar."

"No, no," the mustard jar said. But before it could say more, a police car pulled up outside.

The owner shouted, "Help. I'm being robbed by two clowns and a mustard jar."

133

Two police officers rushed into the gas station. They told the clowns and the mustard jar to put their hands behind their back. The mustard jar couldn't do that because its arms were too short.

The police put handcuffs on the clowns, but they could not put handcuffs on the mustard jar.

The mustard jar tried to tell the cops, "I am not with the robbers," but they didn't believe the jar. They took the jar to the station, along with the two clowns. When they got there, one cop told the clowns and the mustard jar, "Take off those outfits, and take a shower." The clowns took off their outfits, but of course the mustard jar didn't. It tried to tell the police that it wasn't dressed in an outfit, but they didn't believe that.

One cop said, "We'll have to take that outfit off." So they led the mustard jar to the shower room. Then one cop grabbed the lid of the jar and said, "I'll take this part off."

The mustard jar said, "Don't press on that lid too much, or some mustard may squirt out."

The police officers looked at each other and smiled. One cop said, "Did you hear that, Sid? This guy thinks he's got real mustard inside."

"That's silly," the other cop said.

More to come.

133

Mrs. Hudson did not like the pictures that Zelda made for her story about the Snake River. She wanted another artist to make pictures. That artist was named Henry. Henry always seemed to know just what Mrs. Hudson wanted. Henry read this part of the story. "Our raft floated down the river. It was yellow with red stripes." He knew that the raft was yellow with red stripes. But he came to a part of the story that fooled him.

Here's what Mrs. Hudson wrote. "We were on the Snake for an hour before we saw any fast moving water." Henry's picture didn't show the Snake as a river.

1. What was the name of the artist that Mrs. Hudson didn't like?
2. What was the name of the artist she did like?
3. Did Henry know that the Snake was really a river?
4. His picture showed Mrs. Hudson and her friends on ▭.
   - a real snake
   - the Snake River
   - a yellow and red river

163

134

1. war<u>ning</u>
2. wear<u>ing</u>
3. rush<u>ing</u>
4. try<u>ing</u>
5. push<u>ing</u>

1. g<u>ua</u>rd
2. tray
3. key
4. moan
5. locked
6. buddy

1. guy
2. hey
3. toe
4. bench
5. cell

1. whisp<u>e</u>red
2. <u>b</u>ehind
3. <u>a</u>nother
4. great<u>est</u>

The Mustard Jar in Jail

The mustard jar was in jail because the cops thought the mustard jar was a robber. They were trying to take off the mustard jar's outfit. The mustard jar told them not to push on the lid. The jar warned them about what could happen.

One cop was trying to get the lid off, but he couldn't do it. The other cop said, "Let me give you a hand with that lid," and grabbed the plunger. The mustard jar said, "I'm telling you, if you don't stop pushing on that lid, you'll get covered with mustard."

One police officer said, "Ha ha. He thinks that . . ."

A very, very large glop of yellow mustard squirted at that officer. It covered him from head to toe. There was so much mustard on the floor that the cop started to slip and slide. He slid back into the other cop and tried to hold onto him, but all he did was cover the officer with mustard and then pull him down to the floor.

134

Three more cops came running in when they heard all the noise in the shower room. Before they could stop, they ran into the slippery mustard on the floor. Their feet went out from under them. They landed on their seats and slid across the floor on their seats, leaving three big ugly yellow streaks of mustard on the floor.

An hour later, five cops who were covered with mustard put the mustard jar in a cell with the two robbers.

One cop said, "We'll take off your mustard outfit later."

The mustard jar was very sad. He sat on a bench. The other two robbers looked at him for a long time, but they didn't say anything. Finally, one of them said, "Hey buddy, why didn't they take off your silly outfit?"

The mustard jar said, "It's not a silly outfit."

The other robber said, "And why did you come in that gas station when you saw we were there? Why didn't you find your own gas station to rob?"

"I don't rob gas stations," the mustard jar said. "I'm a fire fighter."

One of the robbers almost laughed. He said, "Let me tell you, buddy, you don't look much like any fire fighter I ever saw."

"Me neither," the other one said. "I'll bet you couldn't even hold a fire hose when you're wearing that outfit."

Then the robbers started to laugh. The mustard jar said, "Stop laughing."

More to come.

Birds

Some birds are very small. Some birds are very big. Birds come in all colors and sizes. A bluebird is small. A finch is even smaller than a bluebird. There are birds even smaller than a finch.

A very large bird is an eagle. Eagles live high up in the trees. They make their nests out of tree branches and moss. Sometimes they use other things they find on the ground, like string.

Eagles can fly very fast. They have very long wings. If you're lucky, you may find an eagle feather on the ground when you are walking through a field. Eagles eat fish and mice. Eagles swoop down to the rivers and fields to catch their food.

1. Is a bluebird a big bird or a small bird?
2. Name a bird that is smaller than a bluebird.
3. Is a finch the smallest bird there is?
4. Is an eagle a small bird or a large bird?
5. Where do eagles live?
6. Name two things that eagles eat.

A
1. retell
2. dislike
3. disagree
4. replant

B
1. dollar
2. secret
3. carry
4. guy

C
1. import**ant**
2. **ham**burger
3. **pro**bably
4. **hill**side
5. wo**man**
6. wo**men**

D
1. g**uar**d
2. bucket
3. tray
4. fak**e**
5. cleaner
6. stat**e**

The Mustard Jar Stops the Robbers

The robbers were laughing at the mustard jar, and the jar was ready to cover them with mustard. But just then, a guard with a food tray came up to the cell, and the robbers stopped laughing.

One of the robbers whispered to the other one, "Remember how we'll do this. I'll get sick, and you get the keys."

The guard started to open the door to the cell. Just then one robber fell down on the floor and started to moan. "Oh, I'm sick," he moaned. "Bad sick."

The guard walked over to him and bent down. The other robber snuck up behind the guard and grabbed his keys. Then both the robbers grabbed the guard and made him sit on the bench, next to the mustard jar.

135

The mustard jar said, "What are you guys doing?"

One robber said, "You'll find out real soon."

Both the robbers went out of the cell and locked the door. The mustard jar and the guard were inside the cell. The robbers were outside the cell. And they were laughing. "We're too smart for these guys," one of them said.

The robbers started to run down the hall. The guard said, "They're getting away."

The mustard jar said, "No, they're not."

The jar ran over to the door of the cell and sent a great squirt of mustard through the air. It went over the heads of the robbers and landed on the floor right in front of them.

Before they could stop, they ran into the slippery mustard. Their legs went out from under them, and they slid down the hall on their seats, leaving long ugly yellow streaks of mustard on the floor.

When they stopped, the mustard jar squirted out the greatest glop of mustard that anyone had ever seen. It landed right on top of the robbers and covered them.

Three guards came running down the hall. One of them did not stop in time. Her feet went out from under her, and she went sliding into the robbers. The other guards told the robbers to stand up, but they couldn't do it. They would almost stand up, but then their feet would slide out from under them.

The guards tried to help them stand up, but then the guards started to slip and slide, and down they went into the pile of mustard.

A few minutes later, three mustard covered guards put the two mustard covered robbers back in the cell.

Then the guards let out the guard who was in the cell. That guard told them that the mustard jar was the one who kept the robbers from getting away. So the guards let the mustard jar out of the cell. And they thanked the jar for what it did.

More to come.

The Sun and the Moon

Here is a rule about the sun: The sun comes up every morning. Here's another rule about the sun: The sun goes down every night. Sometimes it's hard to see the sun. On those days, the sun is behind clouds. If the sun is blocked by the clouds, things outside are darker and colder. When the sun feels the hottest, there are not many clouds in the sky.

While the sun is going down for the night, the moon gets brighter. The moon looks brightest at night. Sometimes you can see the moon in the afternoon, but it's not as bright as it is at night.

1. The sun comes up ▓▓▓▓.
2. The sun goes down ▓▓▓▓.
3. Does it feel hotter or colder when the clouds block the sun?
4. When the sun is bright and hot, are there many clouds in the sky?
5. When is the moon the brightest?
6. Can you ever see the moon in the afternoon?

A

1. carry
2. carrying
3. hamburger
4. probably
5. important

B

1. enough
2. wild
3. world
4. worth
5. women

C

1. airplane
2. secret
3. dollar
4. nipping

D

1. popped
2. upset
3. fake
4. state
5. bucket

A Job at Hillside Farm

After the mustard jar stopped the robbers from getting away, the jar got an idea and told it to the chief of police. The jar said, "I'm a good fire fighter, but I would also be a very good cop. Maybe I'll stay here in Big Stone and work as a cop."

The chief said, "You might make a very good cop, but who is going to clean up after you?"

"What do you mean?" the mustard jar asked.

The chief said, "I mean that somebody has to clean up all that mustard in my jail. And somebody has to wash a lot of shirts and pants. And somebody has to clean a lot of shoes."

The mustard jar said, "Oh."

The chief said, "With the mustard that is in my jail right now, you could fix up every hamburger in this state. I've got four workers in the hallway carrying out buckets full of mustard. And they'll probably be carrying out buckets full of mustard three hours from now."

The police chief shook her head and went on. "If you worked here as a cop, I'd need to hire two more people just to clean up after you."

The mustard jar said, "Oh."

Just then, the chief got a phone call. She talked for a while and then hung up. She told the mustard jar, "That was the fire chief of Big Stone. He said that I have to take you to Hillside Farm. It's about four miles outside town."

"What are we going to do out there?" the mustard jar asked.

"I don't have any idea," the chief said. "But we have to get out there right away."

The police chief drove the mustard jar to Hillside Farm. The fire chief was waiting for them. So were two other men and two women. The fire chief told the mustard jar, "These people have heard about the things you do, and they have a very important job for you. They want you to sit out there in the field and make sure that no airplanes try to land on this farm."

"How will I work as a fire fighter if I'm sitting out there in the field?" the jar asked.

"This job is more important than fire fighting," the fire chief said. "If you do a good job of keeping planes from landing here, you may save the world."

The mustard jar asked more questions about the new job, but the chief kept saying, "That's all I can tell you. The rest is a big secret."

Of course, the mustard jar wanted to save the world, so it agreed to sit out in the field and watch for planes. The mustard jar didn't know it, but this job was just a trick to keep the mustard jar from squirting out more mustard.

More to come.

Teeth

Right now, you may have 28 teeth. Grown-up people have 32 teeth. Babies are born with no teeth at all. Your first teeth are called baby teeth because you get them when you're a baby. When the first teeth come in, they do not feel good, and the baby cries.

A lot of kids who are six or seven have teeth missing because they've lost their baby teeth. Soon, bigger teeth grow where baby teeth used to be. These bigger teeth stay with people for the rest of their life, so people should take very good care of their grown-up teeth. You should brush your teeth after each meal.

1. How many teeth do grown-ups have?
2. How many teeth do you have?
3. The first teeth that grow in your mouth are called ▆▆▆▆.
4. As you get older, what happens to your baby teeth?
5. Soon, ▆▆▆▆ will start to grow where baby teeth were.
6. Will these new teeth fall out if you take care of them?

1. sneeze
2. worth
3. enough
4. popped

1. <u>owners</u>
2. <u>cleaners</u>
3. <u>helpers</u>
4. <u>officers</u>

1. elephant
2. suppose
3. waddle
4. wild
5. super

The Mustard Jar Becomes a Dog

A lot of people had heard about the mustard jar, and a lot of them were not happy. The people who were most upset with the mustard jar were the people who sold mustard.

They agreed that if the mustard jar kept squirting yellow mustard all over the place, mustard would not be worth as much as it is worth now.

One person who sold mustard said, "The mustard jar may squirt out a thousand dollars worth of mustard with one squirt. A small jar of our mustard sells for a dollar. If there is mustard all over the place, people are not going to pay a dollar for a small jar of our mustard."

The other people who were not happy with the mustard jar were the people who had to clean up the piles of mustard. Store owners, street cleaners, fire fighters, and police officers complained. One of them said, "We don't have enough mops to clean up those mustard glops."

137

The people who were not happy with the mustard jar got together and made up a plan. They would give the mustard jar a fake job on a farm so the mustard jar would not be near any town or city.

When the Big Stone fire chief told the mustard jar about an important job at Hillside Farm, that was a lie. When people told the mustard jar that it could save the world by doing its job well, that was another lie. They just wanted the mustard jar on that farm so it would not be squirting out thousands of dollars worth of mustard.

The plan worked well for two days. The mustard jar sat in a field and looked for planes. But on the third day, the mustard jar got tired of just sitting.

The mustard jar thought, "No planes come around here. And I would be able to see a plane from other places. I don't have to be in this field to see them."

But the mustard jar didn't feel right about leaving the field because it had told the others that it would stay there. It thought some more. As it was thinking, a dog came by. That dog gave the mustard jar a great idea. The mustard jar said, "I will become a dog. So I won't leave the field. A dog will leave the field."

The mustard jar looked at the dog and began to think, "I am a dog. I am a dog."

Slowly the mustard jar began to change. A stubby yellow tail popped out of the rear end of the jar, and two pointed dog ears popped out of the lid. The stubby yellow arms got paws on the ends and became stubby yellow dog legs. The mustard jar wagged its stubby little tail, said "Bark, bark," and started to walk from the field. The other dog walked with the jar.

The mustard jar was thinking, "We'll just walk back to town and see what's happening. People will look at us and see two dogs walking along." But the mustard jar didn't really look like a dog. It looked like a great big mustard jar with four yellow legs, a yellow tail, and two yellow dog ears.

More to come.

How Animals Move

All animals move. Most land animals use their legs to move from place to place. Dogs, elephants, and people move with their legs.

Birds have legs and wings. Wings help them move in the air, and legs help them move on the ground. Snakes and worms don't have legs or wings. They move their body from side to side and slide along the ground.

Fish don't have legs or wings. By moving their fins and tail, they move through water. Some fish swim as fast as a speed boat.

Some apes use their arms to move. They swing from trees or vines to move around forests.

1. Most land animals use their ▇▇▇▇ when they move from one place to another.
2. Name four animals that use just their legs to move from place to place.
3. Birds have ▇▇▇▇ and ▇▇▇▇ to move with.
4. Name two animals that have no legs or wings.
5. Fish move through water with their ▇▇▇▇ and ▇▇▇▇.
6. What animal uses its arms to swing?

138

A
1. itself
2. nipping
3. sneeze
4. ground
5. tent
6. splat

B
1. carnival
2. couple
3. elephant
4. supposed
5. waddle
6. backward

C
1. super
2. carrying
3. hidden
4. know
5. knew
6. flew

The Mustard Jar Stops at a Carnival

The mustard jar had changed itself into a dog. The jar was walking to the town of Big Stone with another dog. That town was four miles away, and the walk took a long time because the mustard jar did not go very fast on its stubby little legs.

When the jar and the dog were about a mile from town, they started to walk past a farm house. Two big mean dogs rushed out. The dog that had been walking with the mustard jar ran away as fast as it could go. The mustard jar wagged its little yellow tail. It was trying to show the mean dogs that it was friendly. But one of the mean dogs bit that wagging tail.

"Bark, bark," the mustard jar said in its most friendly way. One dog was still nipping at the mustard jar's tail. The other one was starting to nip the jar's yellow ear.

The mustard jar knew that these dogs did not want to be friends. A moment later, the dogs were covered with yellow mustard.

They licked at the mustard, sneezed, and tried to run away. But of course they slipped in the mustard and fell down. "Oooowww," they howled as the mustard jar waddled down the road.

Just outside the town of Big Stone were the fair grounds. Outside the fair grounds was a large sign that said, "World's greatest carnival."

The mustard jar said to itself, "What is this? There was no carnival the last time I was here."

The mustard jar wanted to look around inside the carnival, but the jar didn't want to let any planes land at Hillside Farm. So the jar took a long look at the sky to make sure that no planes were around. Then it went into the fair grounds.

A lot of people were putting up tents and rides like merry-go-rounds. The woman in charge of the carnival was standing near the merry-go-round, talking on a phone. She sounded very upset. "When will that elephant get here?" she said. "We'll have hundreds of people who want to see an elephant, and we don't have one yet . . . ."

The mustard jar stood next to the woman and wagged its yellow tail. She looked at the mustard jar from time to time, but she just shook her head and kept talking on the phone. At last, she put her phone away and turned to the mustard jar. "What do you think you are?" she shouted. "Are you supposed to be a mustard jar or a wild pig?"

Before the mustard jar could answer, she went on. "And why are you in your outfit now? We're supposed to be getting things ready, not waddling around in mustard jar outfits. So get out of that outfit and help those guys who are putting up the merry-go-round."

The mustard jar looked at her, wagged its tail, and said, "Bark, bark."

She shook her head. Then she started to smile. Then she started to laugh. "Okay," she said, laughing. "You are pretty funny. In fact, you are very funny." She started to laugh harder.

More to come.

Animals That Come Out at Night

Some animals come out only at night. When we are at school or playing outside, these animals are sleeping. When it is night, these animals come out to play and look for food. Bats come out at night. Some bats live in dark caves and sleep all day. At night, they fly around looking for bugs to eat. Some foxes also sleep in the daytime. It is too hot for them to come out in the sun. At night, they come out looking for bugs and other small animals to eat.

The moth is another animal that comes out at night. Moths look like butterflies. But butterflies sleep at night. At night, moths fly around looking for food. It's easy to find moths at night. Just turn on a bright light, and the moths will fly to it. They love lights.

1. Do all animals sleep at night?
2. When we are at school, what are bats doing?
3. Name three animals that are awake at night.
4. Why don't some foxes come out in the daytime?
5. How could you find a lot of moths at night?

A

1. knock
2. know
3. knew
4. knee

B

1. sign
2. Anny
3. Hank
4. couple
5. super

C

1. hidd__en__
2. take__n__
3. splatt__ed__
4. hard__ly__
5. ac__tion__

D

1. shoot
2. tiny
3. teeny
4. shack
5. snack
6. stack

Super Mustard

The woman who ran the carnival was named Anny. She was laughing at the mustard jar. The jar was trying not to get mad. Anny said, "Make your tail wag again."

She thought the mustard jar was just a funny act. She wanted to see the jar wag its tail because she thought that was the funny part of the act.

The mustard jar wagged its tail again. Anny howled. By now, some of the other people who worked in the carnival were standing next to her, watching the mustard jar. Anny said to one of them, "What do you think, Hank? Is this act funny or what?"

"It could get one or two laughs," Hank said. "But all it can do is wag its tail. That's not much of an act. If it could do something else that would get a laugh, it would be a good act. But all it can do is . . ."

The squirt of mustard that hit Hank was big enough to knock him back into two workers who were carrying tent poles.

139

Anny was laughing so hard that she could hardly stand up. So were the other people who were watching. Hank was not laughing. He was trying to stand up, but he kept slipping, and Anny kept laughing.

After a while, Anny could talk again. She said, "How did you do that? Where did you have all that mustard hidden?"

The mustard jar looked at her and said, "Bark, bark." Anny started laughing again.

Then she said, "Stop being funny and tell me how you do that thing with the mustard."

The mustard jar said, "I just seem to have all the mustard I need."

She turned to Hank, who looked like a great mustard pile. He was walking toward her. "What do you think, Hank?" Anny said. "Will people laugh at that?"

Hank was mad. "Some people would laugh at anything," he said. "But I don't think people are going to laugh a lot about mustard squirting all over the place. Maybe they would laugh the first time they see it, but how many times are they going to laugh at . . ."

Splat. The glop of mustard that hit Hank sent him flying backward again.

Anny was laughing so hard she had tears running down her cheeks. A couple of the others who were watching were rolling on the ground with laughter.

After everybody finally stopped laughing, Anny walked over to the mustard jar. "What's your name?" she asked. But before the mustard jar could answer, she went on. "Never mind. From now on, your name is Super Mustard, and we're going to work out an act for you that everybody will pay to see."

More next time.

Five Ways of Knowing

People have five different ways of knowing what is happening around them. One way of finding out what is happening is by seeing. We see with our eyes. Another way to know what is happening is by hearing. We hear sounds around us with our ears. A third way is to feel what is around us. We can feel things with our hands, feet, and other body parts. A fourth way we know what is happening is by smelling. We smell smoke and know that something is burning. The fifth way is to use our mouth to taste. Your mouth tells you if food is salty, sweet, sour, or bitter. The five ways of finding out what is happening help keep us safe. We can see danger or hear it, or feel it, or smell it, or even taste it.

1. We use our _____ to see what is happening.
2. We use our nose to _____ what is happening.
3. Can we use our mouth to help us know what is going on?
4. How many ways do we have for finding out what is happening?
5. If food smells bad, could that food be dangerous?

A

1. sign
2. stole
3. purse
4. staring
5. formed

B

1. taken
2. flatter
3. teeny
4. cheering
5. sliding

C

1. shoot
2. shot
3. shack
4. shut
5. shook

The Carnival

The mustard jar didn't know what to do. The jar had told the fire chief that it would keep planes from landing at Hillside Farm. But the mustard jar really wanted to work in the carnival, and it really liked the name Super Mustard.

The jar had a problem. It had already told people it would do one job. But it wanted to take another job.

The jar kept looking at the sky to make sure that no planes were around. The jar hadn't seen a plane in two days, so it said to itself, "I'm going to become Super Mustard, but I'll keep looking out for planes."

That's what the mustard jar did. The next day, there were big signs all around town and around the carnival.

> **SEE SUPER MUSTARD.**
>
> **IT WALKS, IT TALKS,**
>
> **IT SHOOTS OUT MUSTARD.**

Not many people came to the mustard jar's first show, but everybody went away laughing.

At the start of the show, Anny told the people, "Give a big hand for the one and only Super Mustard. Super Mustard will amaze you and make you laugh."

Super Mustard came out dressed like a fire fighter. A clown came out on the other side of the tent with a hot dog. The clown went up to Super Mustard and said, "I need mustard on my hot dog."

Super Mustard sent a teeny tiny squirt of mustard out. A few drops of mustard landed on the hot dog. A few people who were watching the act clapped, but most of them shook their heads.

The clown held up the hot dog and said, "You call that mustard? I like lots and lots of mustard on my hot dog."

The mustard jar squirted out a glop of mustard so big that it covered the hot dog. In fact, it covered the clown. And the clown went sliding backward.

After the mustard jar covered the clown with mustard, the crowd roared with laughter. The mustard jar asked, "Do you need more mustard?" The clown shook his yellow head no.

Just then, a little shack on the other side of the tent started to burn. A clown was inside. "Help," the clown yelled. "My house is on fire."

The mustard jar waddled over to the burning shack. Again, the clown stuck her head out of the window of the shack and yelled, "Help. Put out the fire."

The mustard jar did that. A glop of mustard hit that shack so hard that it knocked the shack over and put out the fire at the same time.

The crowd laughed and cheered.

More next time.

Tree Rings

Very tall trees are very old. You can get an idea of how old a tree is just by looking at it. But if you really want to know how old a tree is, you have to look at the rings inside the tree.

Trees make one ring each year. Rings have a dark part and a light part. The dark part forms in the fall and winter when the tree doesn't grow. The light part forms in the spring and summer when the tree grows.

When a tree is cut down, you can see the rings on the stump. If you count the rings, you know how old the tree is. If the tree has 110 rings, you know that tree is 110 years old.

1. Trees that are very tall are very _____.
2. Can you tell exactly how old a tree is just by looking at it?
3. You can tell exactly how old a tree is by counting its _____.
4. When does the dark part of the ring form?
5. When does the light part of a ring form?
6. If a tree has 11 rings, it is _____ years old.

A

1. buy<u>ing</u>
2. cheer<u>ing</u>
3. star<u>ing</u>
4. men<u>tion</u>
5. na<u>tion</u>

B

1. ton
2. purse
3. stole
4. formed
5. flatter

C

1. <u>every</u>thing
2. <u>some</u>how
3. <u>any</u>where
4. <u>with</u>out

Super Mustard Becomes a Star

The mustard jar had just put out the fire in a burning clown shack. Now Anny went to the middle of the tent and said, "You have seen Super Mustard as a fire fighter. Super Mustard is also a cop who can really stop robbers. Watch this."

Just then a woman in the crowd yelled, "Help, help. Somebody stole my purse." A clown ran from the crowd with the purse. He started to run out of the tent, but before he took five more steps, the mustard jar squirted out a great glop of mustard that landed in front of the robber. The robber ran into the pile of mustard. He slipped and slid and fell on his seat. Then he slid along the ground, leaving an ugly yellow streak.

142

The crowd went wild. The crowd was so loud that more people outside the tent began to wonder what was going on inside. More and more of them came in to watch Super Mustard. Soon all the seats were filled.

Anny went to the middle of the tent. "You have seen Super Mustard as a fire fighter and a police officer, but Super Mustard can turn into other things."

Super Mustard waddled over and stood next to Anny. Anny said, "Watch as Super Mustard turns into a dog." Super Mustard got down on all fours and changed itself into a dog with a stubby tail and yellow ears. Then Super Mustard wagged its tail. Everybody roared with laughter. "Bark, bark," Super Mustard said, and everybody roared again.

Super Mustard stood up, and its ears and tail disappeared. Anny said, "Super Mustard, what would you do if the road was washed out, and you had to warn cars about the danger on the road?"

Super Mustard said, "I would become a stop sign and stand in the middle of the road." The people in the tent shook their heads. Some of them were saying, "Super Mustard couldn't do that." But a moment later, people were staring with wide eyes.

At first the jar got flatter and flatter. Then it changed into the shape of a great big stop sign, and the letters S T O P formed on the sign.

Then the jar fell over because it was too flat to stand up.

"And there you have it," Anny said. "The only yellow stop sign that can put mustard on your hot dog."

When that first show was over, everybody in the crowd was standing and clapping and cheering. The mustard jar was a star.

The next day, some things were different. Anny put the mustard jar in a much bigger tent, and people had to pay a lot more to see the mustard jar's act.

People were lined up for hours to get inside the big tent. Everybody wanted to see Super Mustard.

More to come.

Sand

When you go to the beach, you can see miles and miles of sand. That sand is very old. Sand comes from rocks. The water breaks the rocks into smaller and smaller parts. Over hundreds of years, the waves from the sea turn large rocks into sand. Slowly, the rocks break up into smaller pieces. The more times the waves crash against the rocks, the smaller the rocks become. The crashing of the waves also makes the rocks smooth. You can look at a rock or stone and tell if it has been in the water for a very long time. Rocks that have been in the water do not have sharp corners.

1. On the beach, there are miles and miles of _____.
2. The sand on the beach started out as _____.
3. What turns rocks into sand?
4. The rocks broke up into smaller _____.
5. Does a stone that has been in the sea have sharp corners?
6. Is sand on the beach new or old?

A
1. stor<u>ies</u>
2. bab<u>ies</u>
3. cit<u>ies</u>
4. short<u>en</u>
5. trick<u>ed</u>

B
1. phone
2. vision
3. telephone
4. television

C
1. ton
2. fins
3. chance
4. heap
5. change

D
1. <u>somehow</u>
2. <u>outside</u>
3. <u>newspaper</u>
4. <u>anyone</u>

Super Mustard's Act Gets Better

It didn't take the fire chief and the people who sold mustard very long to find out that the mustard jar wasn't sitting in a field on Hillside Farm. After the mustard jar's first carnival act, there were stories about the mustard jar in the newspapers. There were also stories on television. And everybody talked about the mustard jar. Thousands of people were coming to the town of Big Stone just to see the mustard jar.

Four of the people who sold mustard came to see the fire chief. One woman said, "Somehow, the mustard jar must have found out that we tricked it." She didn't know that the mustard jar was still looking out for planes. She didn't know that the jar waddled outside of the tent every chance it had, so it could look at the sky and make sure that no planes were around. She didn't know that the mustard jar had told two workers to keep looking at the sky and to let the jar know if any planes came by. She thought that the mustard jar knew that they had tricked it.

One of the people who sold mustard told the fire chief, "We must find some way to stop the mustard jar, because if this keeps up, we will have to sell mustard for less than a dollar a jar."

The people who sold mustard didn't know that everybody was talking about mustard more than they ever did before. And they were buying more mustard than they ever did before. Many stores were running out of mustard because so many people were buying it. A lot of kids were saying, "We love mustard."

The chief told the people who sold mustard, "I don't think we can stop the mustard jar, because it is a great star now. I think we'll just have to let the jar know that we are sorry for the trick we played."

Some of the people who sold mustard did not like that plan, but they couldn't think of any way to stop Super Mustard from squirting tons of mustard around, so they agreed with the fire chief's plan.

While they were talking about what they would do, the mustard jar was working very hard. The jar liked to be a star and liked to have people clap and cheer. At first, the jar didn't like it when people laughed, but now the jar knew that the more people laughed, the more they liked Super Mustard.

The mustard jar's act was not always the same. On the second day, Anny added a new part. After the mustard jar turned into a dog and a stop sign, Anny said to the crowd, "Tell me something else you would like to see the mustard jar become."

Somebody wanted to see a chair. So Super Mustard became a yellow chair.

Then a boy said, "Turn into a goldfish."

The mustard jar said, "I can do that, but this goldfish will be yellow." Everybody laughed.

More to come.

Angry Animals — Part 1

Ann had a lot of animals in her yard. She had horses, cows, sheep, and goats. The animals got along with each other very well. Then one day, a mean old man dropped an angry pill in the water. The animals drank the water, and they all became angry. The next morning, Ann had a yard full of angry animals. Those animals were angry at each other and at Ann. The angry horses tried to kick the angry sheep. The angry cows tried to knock over the angry goats. Ann was very upset. She said, "Most of the time my animals get along well. But this morning they are fighting and arguing like the bragging rats."

1. What kinds of animals did Ann have?
2. Most of the time, how well did her animals get along?
3. What made them angry?
4. Did the angry pill make the animals angry at each other?
5. The angry pill also made the animals angry at ▇▇▇▇.
6. What did Ann say her animals were fighting and arguing like?

A

1. world
2. worth
3. worried
4. workers
5. worms

B

1. blushed
2. chief
3. popular
4. sorry
5. station
6. vacation

C

1. shelf
2. shelves
3. leaf
4. leaves

D

1. television
2. telephone
3. women
4. woman

The Mustard Jar Finds Out the Truth

A boy wanted to see the mustard jar become a goldfish. So the jar started to change. First its arms turned into little yellow fins. And its legs turned into a yellow fish tail. Then a big yellow fin popped out of the mustard jar's back. The crowd cheered and clapped.

A girl wanted to see the mustard jar become a telephone. The jar changed into the shape of a yellow phone. Then numbers popped out of the front of the phone. The crowd cheered.

Then the mustard jar said, "Ring, ring," and everybody laughed.

At the end of the show, the crowd cheered for a long time. After the show, the mustard jar spent time talking to people from the newspapers and people from television shows. One of them said, "Do you know that you are the best known star in the world?"

The mustard jar blushed and said, "I just try to be the best mustard jar I can be."

After talking to these people, the jar waddled outside to make sure that there were no planes in the sky. When it went back inside, the fire chief was waiting to see it. The chief said, "I know that you found out about how we tricked you. I just want you to know we are sorry."

The mustard jar said, "How did you trick me?"

The chief said, "You mean you don't know why we wanted you to stay at Hillside Farm?"

"Sure, I know," the jar said. "You wanted me to watch for planes."

The chief shook his head and told the mustard jar about how they made up a fake job. Then the chief said, "I know we were not very smart. And we are sorry."

The mustard jar said, "You did a very mean thing. And you should pay for it. So bring all those people who sell mustard to the carnival, and I will talk to them at the end of my next show."

At the end of the next show, the mustard jar told the crowd, "I want you to meet six people who sell mustard. I have something to say to them."

The fire chief and the people who sold mustard came out to the middle of the tent. The crowd clapped.

The mustard jar said, "These people sell mustard, so they should think about mustard a lot. I'm going to leave them with something that will help them think more about mustard."

The mustard jar squirted out one of the biggest glops of mustard anyone had ever seen. That glop covered the fire chief and all six people who sold mustard.

The crowd roared as the people who sold mustard slipped and slid and fell down in a great heap of people and mustard.

The mustard jar told the people, "Remember to think mustard."

The people who sold mustard did just what the mustard jar said. They went on to sell more mustard than they had ever sold before.

They never tried to trick the mustard jar again. And they helped the mustard jar become the greatest star that ever lived.

The end.

Angry Animals — Part 2

The animals in Ann's yard drank water that had an angry pill in it. The animals became angry. The sheep tried to splash mud on the cows. The goats tried to kick the horses. And all the animals tried to scare Ann. The animals stayed angry for days. Things were so bad that Ann didn't like to feed the animals because they were so mean. They did things to scare her. The horses charged after her. The cows chased her. The sheep splashed mud at her. The goats tried to ram into her. Ann didn't know what to do. She thought, "If my animals don't act nicer than they're acting, I will have to send them to a farm far away."

1. What had made the animals angry?
2. What did the sheep try to do to the cows?
3. What did the goats try to do to the horses?
4. Who did all the animals try to scare?
5. Ann would send her animals away if they didn't act ▬▬▬.
6. Where did Ann think she would send her animals?

Angry Animals — Part 3

Ann thought she might have to send her animals to a farm far away. But one day, a kind old man told Ann, "I think somebody gave your animals an angry pill."

"What can I do to make all that anger go away?" Ann asked.

The old man said, "Give them some happy food."

The old man handed her some big yellow apples and said, "Give each of your animals some slices of these apples. They are good food, and they will make your animals happy."

Ann snuck out that night and put apple slices next to the animals' water. The next morning when Ann got up, she saw that all the slices were gone. She went outside, and all the animals looked at her. They did not seem to be very happy.

Ann was ready to go back inside when all of a sudden the animals smiled. Then they started to play.

Now Ann's animals are very nice to each other. They are also very nice to Ann. Ann makes sure to feed them good food to keep them happy.

1. Who told Ann what was wrong with her animals?
2. What did the kind old man give Ann?
3. When did Ann put apple slices next to the animals' water?
4. Were the animals happy the next morning?
5. Are those animals mean to each other or good to each other?
6. What does Ann feed her animals now?